D1739030

ALSO BY THE AUTHOR

Shark Safari
Florida's Game Fish
Shark Wanted! Dead or Alive

HAL SCHARP

The Freshwater Angler's Clinic

SIMON AND SCHUSTER
NEW YORK

COPYRIGHT © 1979 BY HAL SCHARP
ALL RIGHTS RESERVED
INCLUDING THE RIGHT OF REPRODUCTION
IN WHOLE OR IN PART IN ANY FORM
PUBLISHED BY SIMON AND SCHUSTER
A DIVISION OF GULF & WESTERN CORPORATION
SIMON & SCHUSTER BUILDING
ROCKEFELLER CENTER
1230 AVENUE OF THE AMERICAS
NEW YORK, NEW YORK 10020

DESIGNED BY ELIZABETH WOLL
MANUFACTURED IN THE UNITED STATES OF AMERICA

1   2   3   4   5   6   7   8   9   10

LIBRARY OF CONGRESS CATALOGING IN PUBLICATION DATA

SCHARP, HAL.
THE FRESHWATER ANGLER'S CLINIC.

1. FISHING—MISCELLANEA.   I. TITLE.
SH441.S354   799.1'2   78-26262

ISBN 0-671-24631-3

ACKNOWLEDGMENTS

It would be presumptuous and, indeed, fraudulent of me to take credit for *all* the material in this book. Frankly, I seized the initiative and capitalized on the curiosity of others. So first, I'd like to cast a line of sincere thanks to all the anglers I fished with—the "Joes" and "Janes" who bombarded me with countless questions down through the years. Unknowingly, they furnished the raw material that formed the basis of this book.

I am also indebted to many fishing guides, from Alaska to Florida, whose generous contributions have given this work stature.

Without my wife, Mary, I would certainly have run aground. She not only assisted me in photography, but also patiently deciphered, edited, and transformed my untidy notes into this book.

CONTENTS

CONTENTS

INTRODUCTION

Long before thoughts of writing a book on fishing occurred to me, I became keenly interested in the peculiarities of the game fishes that inhabit the freshwater lakes and streams of our continent. Although several academic courses in ichthyology, and related studies in aquatic ecology, had given me reasonable insights into the behavior and habitats of fish, an aura of mystery continued to surround the creatures. In spite of my academic pursuits, I was often confounded by the personalities of these gamesters—enigmatic, contrary, or just downright ornery!

As my knowledge of angling practices broadened considerably during many years spent wetting lines from Florida to Alaska and California to Maine, my fascination continued to grow. The anglers I guided bombarded me continually with questions. Many questions were sensible, a few bordered on the ridiculous, while others were sufficiently complex or intriguing enough to arouse my curiosity. When I couldn't answer their questions (or mine!), I became obsessed with finding the solutions. I plunged into further studies and converted my boat into a veritable floating laboratory where I conducted some highly eccentric research. Even close friends and outdoor chroniclers frequently expressed bewilderment at my "kooky"—but often successful—experiments.

Because I am methodical by nature, I meticulously recorded all the questions and my findings, amassing a mountain of data and notes in the process. Eventually, I realized I had accumulated a mine of fresh, factual information predicated upon queries from hundreds of frustrated anglers. Some of these questions had never been discussed in contemporary angling literature before, but now that I had the answers—or most of them—the idea of writing this book sprang to life.

Since my notations numbered in the thousands, my first task was to reduce the size of my enormous aggregation. Then, as I collated the material, I refined many questions and answers to make them more objective and meaningful. To give the angler confidence, I injected new, proved techniques and tested stratagems; to increase his productivity, I emphasized the vital link between natural science and fishing; to improve his expertise, I included the latest advances in modern tackle technology.

This question-and-answer approach to a book on fishing is a new concept. Fishermen (normally a patient breed) tend to lose their patience when they must wade through a profusion of miscellany before they locate answers to specific questions. My short, snappy format is far removed from the conservative, textbook presentation. There's no mystique here. All answers are to the point. When the reader has a question, he simply consults the master index for his subject. There he will find the question he is seeking, and a flip of the pages locks him in, quickly and directly, to his answer.

There was another practical reason for using this format. It will appeal to any angler who has only a vague idea of what he wants to know, which he can't quite put into words. It is easy for him to become discouraged and lost in obscure trivia while plowing through page after page, hoping to spot the answer to his unformulated question. He may even forget what he was looking for! With this format, however, he can nail down his question in seconds and find an immediate answer.

On the other hand, the casual browser will want to read this book for its entertainment value. As one question leads to another, he will be enticed to read on—if only to check his knowledge against the author's. While it may not make him a champion, it will stimulate a desire to grab his rod and charge down to the nearest fishing hole!

The subject of freshwater fishing is vast and, at times, so perplexing as to create thousands of questions in the minds of anglers. However, I feel I have provided the reader with an excellent selection of those questions asked most often (including some that *should* have been asked!), representing a realistic cross section of angling knowledge.

Paradoxically, it's fortunate that some questions may never be answered! If we had *all* the answers, there would be no mystery; the angler would lose his incentive; the search for new techniques would cease; hooking and landing a game fish would no longer be a valid sporting event. But as long as some of nature's eccentricities continue to puzzle us, challenges will develop and expand, along with the angler's inquisitiveness . . . and his questions!

HAL SCHARP

PART ONE

The
Quarry

————————

1

The Basses

SMALLMOUTH BASS

What is the world rod-and-reel record for smallmouth bass?

Records compiled by the staff of *Field & Stream* magazine list an 11-pound-15-ounce smallmouth caught at Dale Hollow Lake, Kentucky, in 1955.

What is the range of the smallmouth bass?

Smallmouths are found in the Great Lakes area, southern Canada, and south into Tennessee and Arkansas. As a result of transplantation, they are found in the New England sector and in some southern rivers and reservoirs. Some clear streams and lakes in the Northwest boast about the size of their smallmouths, especially those caught in the Snake River in Washington.

What are some of the smallmouth's favorite natural foods?

Minnows, shrimp, crayfish, insects, and hellgrammites.

Why do smallmouth bass put up a better scrap than their near cousins, the largemouths?

Anglers are of the opinion that it is because their habitats are different. Smallmouths are more difficult to please and are found in cooler, faster-moving, and cleaner water than large-mouths. Largemouth bass seem to be able to adapt to environments that are totally unsuitable for smallmouths.

Where will I be most likely to find smallmouth bass in streams and swift-moving rivers?

Their favorite spots are near semisubmerged boulders and in pools at the foot of riffles or rapids.

What kind of habitat do smallmouths prefer in lakes?

They like clean, rocky shorelines containing areas of weeds, sandy or gravel bars, and deep, rocky ledges.

Where can I find hellgrammites, and how do I rig them for smallmouth bass?

Hellgrammites (the larvae of the dobsonfly) are often available at bait and tackle shops in areas where active bass fishing exists. If you're hunting for them, they can be found around and under the rocks of shallow, shady streams. If you are storing them for a short time, keep them in a pail or can containing grass or grape leaves and place them in a cool spot.

Hellgrammites have a prominent collar. Insert the hook as shallowly as possible under the collar, and expose the point of the barb so that they can't slip off. Fish them on the bottom where smallmouths are suspected, but don't let them crawl under rocks.

What temperatures do smallmouth bass prefer in lakes?

The most comfortable water-temperature range for smallmouths is 60 to 70 degrees F. They move into shallow water at 60 degrees and really like 67 better than any other temperature. They'll stay in 67-degree water regardless of food availability, but will make occasional forays to other zones that contain food when they get hungry enough.

If I could fish anywhere in North America, where would I find a real smallmouth hot spot?

Among the best are the connecting harbors along the eastern shoreline of Lake Michigan near the northern end: Garden and Hog Islands in the Beaver Island group; Pentwater Lake, in the upper half of the Lower Peninsula; and Wangoshance Point, located in the Wilderness State Park near the Straits of Mackinac.

What happens to smallmouth bass when the temperature in lakes rises above 67 degrees?

Smallmouths gradually retire to the deeper rock ledges; highly aerated, shaded water; deep eddies; and deeply undercut banks. They stop feeding during the day and forage only at night, early in the morning, and evenings.

At some of the northern lakes along the Canadian border when a cold spell sets in, the water becomes chilled and the smallmouths leave the shallows. Any suggestions?

If weather permits, you'd better get a boat and hunt for the bass. Try trolling deep along the ledges and drop-offs. Since it takes quite a while for the deep water to chill, the bass are probably down there.

How can I locate smallmouths in a strange river that I know contains a good population?

If the local bait dealers are reluctant to share their secrets, just sit by the river in the evening and watch for bass to feed. You should be able to see them rising to floating insects or chasing other aquatic life such as frogs and minnows. Try to match your lure to what they're feeding upon. This takes time, but it's a good step in the right direction.

Is there any difference in the dispositions and game qualities of the smallmouth and largemouth bass?

Smallmouths are more finicky eaters, warier, and spookier. They're fussier about water clarity and will not tolerate muddy or polluted water. They are also less tolerant of temperature variations and will move where it is more comfortable at the slightest change.

As compared with largemouths, pound for pound, smallmouths exhibit noticeably more stamina and endurance. This may be due to their clean living habits and gourmet appetites.

By what other names are smallmouth bass known?

Other names are bronze bass, swagobass, welshman, yellow bass, tiger bass, brown bass, gold bass, and redeye.

What is the life-span of a smallmouth bass?

If he isn't captured by rod and reel, and if pollution doesn't suffocate or poison him, a smallmouth could live to 15 years. A 10-year-old weighs roughly 4 pounds and will measure

about 18 inches. Unlike the largemouth, with its greatly distended belly, the smallmouth manages to retain its streamlined figure.

**When smallmouths have retreated to deep water, what should
I use for bait?**

Use any of the diving plugs, spinners, or spoons. Also, you
can try drifting or anchor fishing with minnows, hellgrammites, night crawlers, or crayfish in deep water.

What are some good fly-rod lures for smallmouth bass?

These bass are strong on insects, so lures imitating crickets,
grasshoppers, beetles, and moths are best when you're fishing
at dusk or in late afternoon. A big, fat night crawler is tempting
to smallmouths at night.

Reliable flies are the Woolly Worm, Muddler Minnow, and
streamers made of marabou. When dry flies are indicated, the
Delaware Bug, Devil Bug, and Cooper Bug are all excellent.
Floating rubber bugs, made in both sinking and floating
models such as the Water Hag and Water Cricket, are also
killers. Patterns made by small frogs in the quiet pools of a
bass stream won't last long, especially in the evening.

What is the best live bait for catching smallmouth bass?

Crickets are the choice of most anglers who do a lot of smallmouth bass fishing. Since a cricket is a tiny morsel, a small
hook should be used. If there is little current, insert the hook
under the collar of the cricket with the point facing the rear. If
the current might be swift enough to tear the cricket from the
hook, better run the hook through the body.

If I can't purchase crickets, what is the best way to catch them?

The night before you go fishing, make a trap out of an old loaf of bread. Cut the bread in half and remove the soft part from each half. At one of the ends, make a 1½-inch circular hole. Place the two halves together and secure them with rubber bands or string. Leave the trap in a field of high grass. In the morning, shake your bait out through the hole into a glass fruit jar. Don't forget to punch holes in the jar cover for ventilation.

LARGEMOUTH BASS

What is the best way to distinguish a smallmouth bass from a largemouth bass?

The chief difference is in the location of the jaw joint. When

The largemouth bass, one of America's favorite game fishes, can be distinguished from the smallmouth by its jaw joint which extends well beyond the rear of its eye. (HAL SCHARP)

the mouth of the smallmouth is closed, the rear end of the jaw joint is directly below the eye; on the largemouth, it extends back of the eye. The cheek of the smallmouth has from 12 to 17 rows of small scales, while the largemouth has no more than 12. In the smallmouth the dorsal fin is not deeply notched, but the dorsal of a largemouth will often appear as two separate fins.

Normally the smallmouth bass is the smaller of the two species and seldom averages more than 1 or 1½ pounds, although in some special areas 4- and 5-pounders can be found.

In the hot summer months I slow-troll in deep water using a deep-diving plug. I'm sure my catch would be better if I could keep the plug from snagging the bottom weeds. Any suggestions?

Remove the hooks from your plug so that it can snake through the weeds without fouling. Tie your favorite bass bug or floating plug (hooks intact) to a dropper line and attach the end to your trolling line about 3 feet above the hookless plug. Your new buoyant lure will now wiggle along the top of the bottom growth.

Why can't the smallmouth and largemouth bass be raised artificially like other game fishes bred in hatcheries?

They can. However, extracting their eggs and milt in hatcheries would result in injuries to their sex organs. Therefore, in order to spawn, bass must build their own nests and lay their eggs to hatch naturally. After the eggs are fertilized by the male and are hatched, the young fry are scooped up by the attendants and transferred to rearing ponds.

Are the feeding habits of bass affected by changes in barometric pressure?

There is no proof that pressure variations have a direct effect on the feeding habits of bass or other freshwater fishes.

Barometric-pressure changes *will* cause movements in surface insect larvae which, in turn, might spark some feeding activity by the fish. There are indications that fish in shallow bays and rivers may be sensitive to barometric changes, but the mechanism by which they are able to sense an approaching change is still unknown.

How long do black bass live before they die of natural causes?

About 10 years. Many bass actually starve to death in spite of a steady food supply. They develop cataracts that eventually blind them—making it impossible for them to find food. They usually hole up in some dark place on the bottom, calmly accept their fate, and expire.

To what family of fishes do the black basses belong?

Black bass are not true bass. They are members of the sunfish family along with bluegills, crappies, warmouths, and redears.

How fast can black bass swim?

When compared with other gamesters, bass are slow swimmers which average only 10 to 15 miles per hour. But their lack of speed is overshadowed by their strength and acrobatics which make them ideal sport fish on light tackle.

At what time of year are largemouths more likely to take a bait?

In the spring, when the water temperature begins to rise. Their metabolism accelerates and they like to linger in the shallows prior to their spawning periods. Then, of course, they are more aggressive when competition is in the area and, later, become protective while guarding their nests.

What artificial lures do expert anglers prefer when fishing for smallmouth and largemouth bass?

The choice of lures depends primarily on the habitat of the bass. For instance, in weed and lily-pad beds, a lure with one or more weedless hooks should be used. The famous Johnson Weedless Spoon with a pork-rind strip has been a favorite lure for many years. Also, a lure or artificial frog with a weedless

A variety of lures made specifically for bass. Hair bugs and poppers with rubber legs are especially effective fly-rod lures when worked slowly in quiet water. (HAL SCHARP)

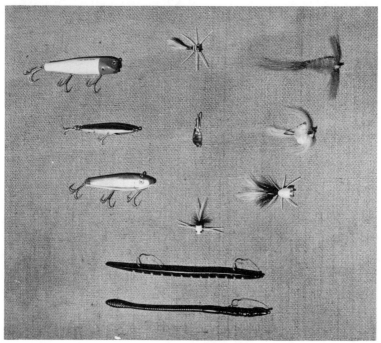

hook is popular, since bass like to lurk among the lily pads where frogs live.

All species of bass love large night crawlers, and since the inception of the plastic worm, this lure has become a real killer when used properly. It is manufactured with or without hooks and comes in a variety of colors and sizes. Experts usually prefer the black plastic worm without hooks so that they can place their own hooks in a strategic position to match the striking characteristics of their quarry.

During the spring nesting period, when male bass are guarding their eggs or young in the shallows, top-water lures or commotion plugs are excellent. The antagonized males usually strike hard when the plugs are lobbed directly over the nest.

There are countless lures on the market that will take bass, but most are caught strictly by the proper movements which are imparted to the lure by the angler.

Any tackle shop located near good bass water will have a wide, colorful selection to tempt the angler. It is the wise angler, however, who can glean from the proprietor some honest information as to which lures are actually catching bass at that particular time in that specific locality.

What is the "slip sinker" method of rigging plastic worms, and how is it accomplished?

This is the method preferred by experts. It has several advantages that outweigh all other methods. The sinker, a cone-shaped piece of lead (which conforms to the tapered worm head) with a hole through the center, comes in various weights from ⅛ ounce to 1 ounce. It is threaded onto the line, where it slips up and down freely. When a bass takes the plastic worm, the sinker remains motionless as the line moves through it—taking the weight off the worm so that it feels more natural to the bass.

The added weight of the sinker helps the angler execute longer casts. Also, because of the freedom of the sinker on the line, it is easier to dislodge the worm from obstructions by jigging the line to work it loose. The entire rig is practically weedless and can be fished without becoming fouled.

Special sharp 4/0 or 5/0 worm hooks are used (with a bend in the shank just behind the eye). Insert the point into the center of the head of the worm. Work the point of the hook up the worm about ½ inch and then break through outside. Now pull the hook until the eye is buried in the end of the worm's head. Then bury the barb inside the worm about halfway, keeping the worm straight so that it won't twist the line when it is retrieved.

What is "bass bugging"?

This is fishing with a variety of fly-rod lures called "bugs" designed expressly for bass. All bass bugs are floating lures and are made to imitate natural baits such as frogs, mice, dragonflies, bees, and moths. Some bugs, called popper bugs, are made to create a sound when the line is retrieved in jerks or the tip of the rod is jiggled. The purpose of the sound is to attract bass or panfish.

While trolling for bass, I have to use an oversized reel and a heavy rod to accommodate the 300 to 400 feet of line it takes to get my lure down deep. Can you suggest lighter tackle that would produce the same results?

Apparently you've tried using drails or other types of lead sinkers and found them impractical from a sporting point of view. And a lunker bass can easily be lost as he shakes his head during his jumps. The hooks will pull out eventually as the heavy lead sinker flies off in another direction.

Ask your favorite tackle supplier about lead-core lines. There are several kinds on the market, and they come in various line tests. Some are made of tough hand-braided nylon sleeve and are coded to indicate depths. That is, the length of the line is identified at intervals of 50 feet. While you formerly would require 300 feet to get your line down to the 25-foot level at normal trolling speed, the lead-core line trolled at the same speed reaches the same depths but requires only about 75 to 100 feet.

There are some new lead-core lines on the market that are coated with urethane. These allow the line to sink faster and cut down on wear and tear.

Lead-core lines are usually packed 100 yards per spool, two spools per box, and should give you more than enough latitude for short trolling lines.

What are the most productive times to fish for bass?

At night. Most aquatic creatures are on the prowl and feeding. Worms and crustaceans leave their hiding places in search of food. Reptiles such as lizards, snakes, frogs, and turtles all hunt at night. Bass know this instinctively and will feed more aggressively during the night than in the daytime. Your catch will be greater—but you won't enjoy it as much as daylight fishing. At night you're liable to tangle with shoreline or shallow-water vegetation because of poor visibility. You really can't see much of what you're doing, especially if your tackle becomes snarled when you're making a proper bait presentation. And above all, the spectacle of a hooked bass jumping and splashing in the sunlight is a lot more fun than feeling the action without being able to observe it.

The early-morning and evening hours are fairly productive, much more than midday. During the daylight hours, bass are always looking for cover along the shoreline if they're not skulking in the deep holes during the hot summer. Bass love to lurk in the shadows of shoreline contours and vegetation, waiting for their meal to swim by. When the sun is at its lowest in the sky, a longer shadow is cast by any object. An angler is likely to find more bass lying in long shadows than in little or no cover.

In casting plugs for bass, what's the best method to retrieve them to create maximum attraction?

Virtually every manufacturer of test-proved plugs (especially the "killer" models) accompanies its lures with written directions and instructions on their use that will result in successful strikes.

There are surface plugs, underwater plugs, and plugs that float but will dive when retrieved. Almost all plugs have a device or are shaped in a manner that gives them the action most appealing to bass. You must, however, learn how to retrieve these plugs to obtain maximum appeal. For instance, a "plunker" model, if retrieved slowly and steadily, will not do what it was designed for. If you execute an erratic retrieve with short, quick jerks of the rod tip, the plug will pop, gurgle, and "plunk." The action and sounds are attractive to all bass and even muskies and pike.

Another popular model known as the "darter" is designed for diving, darting, and jumping out of the water. All these surface and semisurface plugs are called "commotion plugs," and each one has its particular function.

Underwater plugs are sometimes sinkers or floaters with a metal lip that causes them to wiggle and wobble. They are easier to use, since the actions or proper movements take place automatically on any kind of retrieve. This does not mean that their use is practical at all times. If the bass are deep, one of these is the plug for them, but don't use it in shallow water.

When using an artificial worm on bass, when and how hard should I set the hook?

When the worm enters the water, you should maintain a constant watch over the point of entry—especially if the water is shallow. Also, be on the alert for the faintest change in the feel of your rod. As soon as you feel a "touch" indicating that a bass has taken the worm, set the hook immediately with full force. As some old-timers put it, "Hit 'im hard enough to pull his head off!"

This theory is a complete reversal of the slow striking methods commonly practiced in the early 1950s when the first plastic worms made their appearance.

Most bass anglers believe that when a bass (especially a largemouth!) opens his big mouth, he engulfs a tremendous amount of water along with the worm. If he's too suspicious of the offering, he expels it quickly before you can set the hook.

A fairly stiff rod should be used for fast and deep hook-setting methods.

Since I use a lot of fly-rod poppers for bass, I wonder why some produce strikes and others don't and, when I do get a strike, I miss setting the hook. What should I look for in design and shape?

There are two important things to consider when you're making or purchasing bass poppers. First, they must lie on the water with the rear and hook submerged well below the surface. This creates a louder "pop" when you make a retrieve. Second, the popper should be made on a fairly long hook. The hook should sit well aft of the body so that a bass is not forced to engulf the entire lure before he can be hooked.

What is the best way to fish for bass in heavy weeds and grass?

A good deal depends upon the nature of the obstructions. Is the grass too heavy to pull a weedless lure through? If the water is too deep, a bass lurking on the bottom in thick weed growth might see your lure—even strike it—but you'd never get him out. It's best to present your lure close to the edge of the weeds but in deep water. There you might have a chance of pulling out into open water for the struggle. A stiff rod and strong line really help in these situations.

A worthwhile trick is to cast a weedless spoon with a pork strip or an 8- or 10-inch pork eel secured to a ½-ounce weedless spinner into the heavy grass. Retrieve it as fast as possible so that it barely touches the water and slides quickly through the grass. When it reaches the open water, slow down a little and give the bass a chance to grab it after he has chased it through the weeds. You should make sure your boat is 20 feet or more away from the edge of the grass. This method requires long casts, and you really don't expect to hook one while he is running through the grass. All you want to do is antagonize him and get him to follow the lure out to open water.

I get a lot of bass strikes when I use a plastic worm and light spinning rod, but I can't keep the fish on the hook. What am I doing wrong?

Since you're getting strikes, your technique is okay. Your trouble must be with your tackle—your rod is probably too flexible. Plastic worms require a stiff rod so that you can drive the hook fast through a balled-up bunch of worms in the bass's mouth. Don't forget, when a bass picks up a worm, it is usually sucked in and tangled around the hook. Even though the hook is needle sharp, it takes a hard, fast jerk to force the hook through one or more coils of plastic before it enters the flesh (or tough membrane) of a bass's jaw.

Unfortunately, you'll lose casting distance with a stiffer rod—but you'll catch more bass!

I notice that some anglers don't bother to use a landing net when boating their bass. I can never get close enough to see how they accomplish this, but I know they use their bare hands. Isn't this dangerous?

The oversized lower lip of a bass makes a perfect finger-hold. You simply stick your thumb into his mouth and get a firm grip on the lower jaw. Bend the jaw downward as much as possible as you lift him from the water. This paralyzes him momentarily and eliminates his fussing about or jumping out of your grasp.

Special care should be taken, however, if a hook is exposed in his jaw—especially the treble variety found on plugs. If

If you don't use a net, the next-best way to land a bass is to grasp it by the lower lip. This will paralyze the fish momentarily— but watch out for those hooks!
(ILLINOIS DEPT. OF CONSERVATION)

this is the case, after your bass is played out alongside your boat, slide the palm of your hand under his belly and lift him slowly into the boat. Surprisingly, the bass will lie docile in your hand. He is temporarily immobilized because his own weight is pressing his stomach against his spinal cord. Once your bass is in the boat, use a rag (I like terry-cloth towels lifted from my wife's linen closet) to grasp him firmly and then remove the hook.

I'm after lunker bass. What is the best bait, and how do I rig a presentation?

Live shiners (roach or golden minnows)—big ones, 6 to 10 inches—are your best bait. Sometimes they are hard to find, since few commercial suppliers provide them. Some resorts catch their own or buy them from local fishermen. You can catch your own using a cane pole, a light line, and a very small cork. Use tiny balls of moistened bread on a No. 10 or 12 hook. To attract the minnows, chum them with cereal products or crushed crackers.

Shiners can be hooked three different ways—each for a special reason. If you wish your bait to swim deep, insert the hook through the back (carefully avoiding the spine) but to the rear of the dorsal fin. For a shallow offering, the hook must be inserted through the back but in front of the dorsal fin. Incidentally, these two methods can employ the use of a treble hook, which has some advantage in ensuring striking success. However, if the area is congested with weeds or hyacinths, treble hooks are troublesome.

The third method is hooking the shiner through both lips, which will keep it alive a long time. With a slack line the shiner can swim freely either deep or shallow—making it a very natural and tantalizing offering. When Mr. Lunker makes his grab, strike immediately!

Professional bass guides prefer a lively 6-inch roach minnow for lunker bass. (HAL SCHARP)

What can I use to improve the odor of pork-rind strips to make them more effective?

An old trick used by the pros is to soak the strips in cod-liver oil. If they get too soft and begin to tear apart, use more brine to toughen them.

What is the best way to hook a large night crawler when I'm casting for bass with a fly rod?

In order for the night crawler to appear natural by crawling along the bottom, the point of the hook should be inserted into the worm's head. Bury the point and barb an inch away from the head. If the bottom is congested with weeds or grass, use a weedless hook with a sensitive wire guard.

I hook, and lose, a lot of bass in lily pads. Is there any technique that I can apply to improve my landings?

Sounds as if you're in the right place but with the wrong tackle. You'll have to use a heavier line and stiff rod to pull the bass through the heavy growth. Or, as soon as you hook your bass, you might try jerking him to the surface and pulling hard enough to skitter him along the top of the pads into open water. Naturally, these methods don't give bass a sporting chance—so you'll have to draw the line where sportsmanship ends and meat fishing begins.

Why are Florida bass larger than those found in the northern states?

Florida bass attain such husky dimensions because of their environment—a habitat that is ideally suited for their propagation and growth. The growth of northern bass is restricted, in part, by the longer period of cold weather. Because of severe climatic changes, feeding activities and food supplies are limited when compared with those of southern bass which enjoy suitable water temperatures and a continuous food supply practically the year around. Naturally, growth rates are affected.

Georgia and Florida bass weighing 8 pounds or more usually have huge, distended bellies that give these fish a peculiar appearance of sluggishness. This indicates that they're well fed but does not necessarily reduce their true game characteristics.

Unfortunately for Florida, Georgia presently lays claim to the official world's-record bass caught on rod and reel. This beauty weighs 22 pounds 4 ounces and was caught in 1952. Georgia bass thrive in ecological conditions almost identical to those of Florida bass.

What is "jigger fishing" for bass?

"Jigger fishing" is growing in popularity, although it is hardly a sporting method of catching game fish. It is so effective that some states have prohibited its use. It is used mostly for catching bass and panfish.

The angler uses a very long bamboo pole with its tip bent so that it drags in the water. A heavy line only 15 to 24 inches long attached to a lure, usually a plug, is secured to the bent tip of the pole. The line trails behind the pole tip a few inches below the surface while the tip drags in the water. As the lure moves slowly along the edge of the weeds or lily pads, the fisherman taps the butt end of the pole to create vibrations and sounds which are transmitted from the pole tip to the water. This creates an attraction to fish and causes them to rise and strike.

When do largemouth bass spawn, and what is their rate of growth?

A few largemouths spawn in their second year, but most begin in their third year. Spawning usually starts in the spring when the water temperature reaches about 60 degrees. If bottom conditions are suitable, eggs will hatch in 7 to 16 days when the water temperature reaches about 65 degrees in depths of 18 to 36 inches. Although bass prefer a sandy or fine-gravel bottom, they will spawn in deeper water if the shallows are murky. The spawning season lasts about 2 months, depending upon the climatic conditions.

Their growth depends upon their environment and food supply. Northern bass become dormant during the long winter months, when food is scarce. Naturally, low temperatures and the lack of food hinder a fish's growth rate. These fish might take from 2 to 3 years to reach 2 pounds and 6 or 7 years to reach 5 pounds.

In southern states, bass grow much faster because of the longer period of warm weather, which makes the water rich with plankton and minerals. Under these conditions, bass will grow to almost 2 pounds during their first year. They'll gain about one pound a year for the next 2 or 3 years. From then on, they'll average ½ pound yearly. According to their scale readings, Deep South bass average 5 pounds during their fourth year.

If the male bass is more active than the female and takes over all the chores of raising their young, exactly what does he do?

Since the parental instinct of the male is much greater than that of the female, he does a lot more than raising the young. When the spawning season approaches in the spring, the male leaves his group or school and hunts for a suitable location to build a nest, usually in about 3 feet of water. If the water is too cool because of an early-spring chill, then he builds a nest in shallower water, sometimes only 18 inches deep, to absorb the sun's warmth.

The male then creates a saucer-shaped depression on the bottom by fanning with his tail. This exposes coarse gravel and pebbles and helps keep the future eggs in place. After completing his task, the male leaves the nest to seek a suitable female and persuade her to deposit her eggs in his homesite.

After she completes her deposit, the male may fertilize the eggs immediately or drive her away and court one or more other females for additional eggs.

After the eggs are fertilized (the male hovers over the eggs and releases a cloud of milt which descends upon the eggs), he stands constant guard against predators and fans the eggs occasionally to keep the nest free of debris. At this point, he refuses all food while guarding 5,000 to 20,000 eggs.

Depending upon the water temperature, the eggs hatch in 5 to 9 days. When the young begin to swim, the father herds them into schools where they can hide and feed in the dense vegetation. Intruders upon this domestic scene are devoured or chased away. When the young bass are able to forage for themselves, they scatter instinctively and leave the father for good. By now, the male has a ravenous appetite and begins his hunt for food to satisfy the intense hunger induced by his long vigil on the nest.

Are real live night crawlers better bait for bass than artificial worms? If not, please explain the proper techniques for fishing plastic worms.

Yes indeed, if they're available and if you can keep them alive long enough to be effective. Unfortunately, most of the time fresh, wiggling night crawlers are not available. However, the plastic worm is so effective when worked properly that most skilled anglers don't bother searching for live worms.

The plastic worm is of little value if it is not retrieved properly. Patience and concentration on the part of the angler are necessary to make a bass become interested enough to gobble it.

After casting the worm, you must allow it to flutter to the bottom by twitching the rod tip while the worm is sinking. If a strike occurs before the worm settles to the bottom, the hook must be set immediately. When the worm is lying on the bottom motionless or when it is being slowly retrieved is the only time a bass should be allowed to mouth it before you set the hook. A bass will gobble a free-floating or sinking bait, but when a bait is lying on the bottom or being retrieved, he usually nibbles or mouths it first before sucking in the entire offering.

A plastic worm must be retrieved very slowly. In order to simulate the natural movements of a live one, the plastic worm must be made to wiggle and undulate while slithering over the bottom. The retrieve is made in a go-and-stop fashion, moving along the bottom about 6 to 12 inches at a time. Sometimes a not-so-hungry bass is curious enough to follow the worm all the way to the boat or shoreline. Therefore, as the worm reaches the end of the retrieve, it should be jigged slowly up and down a few times before you remove it from the water. An experienced bass fisherman will allow himself at least 2 or 3 minutes to retrieve a plastic worm after making a 50- or 60-foot cast.

What are some of the behavior patterns of bass, and where can I find them during the hot summer months and in the winter?

When bass are hungry, they'll prowl around looking for food. But when they're not feeding, they have a distinct area where they school together. During the extreme hot months they'll congregate in deep depressions or holes, with the small bass hovering over schools of larger bass. Skin-diving biologists have observed bass lying at different levels, from 15 to 30 feet with no fish between the groups. Obviously, presenting your bait near the bottom will more likely produce the lunkers.

Hot-weather bass are hard to find, but real effort will locate their "comfort zones." Although they may go several days without feeding, they can be provoked into taking a bait. During the early morning, especially at dawn, is the best time. They can be found in 20 to 40 feet of water on or near the bottom, near dense weeds. Deep underwater springs too are excellent areas in which to find schools of bass enjoying the cool temperature. Cold-water springs can be located with a thermometer or by observation of the water surface early in the morning when a mist occurs directly above the spring.

A modern bass boat makes it possible for you to reach your quarry lurking under tree stumps and overhanging brush. Note the electric trolling motor that can ease you *quietly* within casting range of a bass's habitat. (JOHNSON MOTORS)

Respecting local season restrictions, the best time to catch more lunker bass is during the cooler months, from September to April, when bass are much more concentrated. Small forage fish are scarce, so live fish or artificial plugs are accepted readily. During the winter there are particularly good spells when bass respond quickly to a bait. These take place when the water warms up temporarily after a cold period. It isn't the temperature itself but, rather, the sudden change. Better fishing can be expected when the rise of temperature is fast and great. Water will then reach its maximum temperature between 3 and 4 in the afternoon, making it the best time to fish on cold days when the sun is shining.

In your opinion, what causes a bass to charge a lure?

There are several reasons. Bass, like most other creatures, possess traits such as hunger, greed, paternal instincts, and even fear of competition. Did you ever notice how distended their bellies often become? They actually overstuff themselves! Overeating can be a result of greed or a fear of competitors—other bass foraging in their territories. So they'll charge a lure, not because they are hungry, but to keep the other guy from getting it.

Naturally, when hunger makes itself felt, they'll make a grab at anything resembling food. Also, a male bass guarding his nest will strike at practically any intrusion that represents a threat to the safety of his young. Paternal instincts are pretty strong in bass. Many anglers who are aware of this characteristic make a point of searching for nests in the shallows and casting commotion-type plugs to the apprehensive bass.

I'm confused by the great number of bass lures offered in tackle shops all over the country. Do these lures, some of which border on the ridiculous, really catch bass? If so, why?

I'd say so, without reservation! Since lure manufacturing is big business, most companies make serious efforts to research their products before marketing them. This means field testing—or to put it more accurately, just plain fishing. When they find one that's a "killer," they market it—regardless of how ridiculous it may appear. Don't forget, each lure is packaged with explicit instructions for its use. The manufacturers really want you to catch fish with their lures so you will brag about your catches and create even more sales.

Bass lures are designed for any number of varied situations and conditions that a bass fisherman may encounter. Weather and water are two factors that determine the designs of lures. The time of year is important also, when water temperature and depth dictate the kind of lure that will be more effective. For example, during the hot summer months when the water is warm, you must locate your bass in deeper water. This means deep-running lures. Here again, different-styled lures are designed to perform a specific job.

Habitats and existing food supplies are two other variables. The lure that works in one lake won't necessarily catch fish in another. If bass are feeding on minnows, you should use spoons that simulate minnows; if they're feeding on frogs, okay, pick a lure that resembles a frog.

Regardless of how ridiculous it may seem to you, manufacturers do a darn good job of designing lures that look like worms, crickets, hellgrammites, mice, snakes, birds, and all the other natural foods of bass.

In a nutshell, the trick is to use the right lure at the right time!

If you could choose only four artificial bass lures to use with your spinning tackle, which ones would you pick?

First, a surface-commotion plug—the kind that makes a lot of noise and disturbance on the water. This is particularly effective for big male bass hovering over their nests.

Then, during the hot summer months, I'd need a deep-diving plug or weighted spoon for trolling, to locate bass schooling in the cool depths.

In the early-morning hours, a weedless lure such as the Johnson Silver Minnow, or an Uncle Josh Pork Frog, on a Weedless Kicker is just right to fish the shallow weed beds and lily pads.

Finally, for my evening fishing, I'd take a black plastic worm with slip sinker and single weedless hook—every time.

My favorite wilderness lake has always produced plenty of largemouth bass. Now the bass are scarcer every year. There is no contamination and no overgrowth of plant life, but I *have* noticed a sharp increase in the panfish population. Would this have anything to do with the scarcity of bass?

Definitely. Game fish, such as bass, normally feed upon the

panfish that constitute a major part of their diet and, therefore, keep the panfish population under control. Obviously, this ideal balance has been severely upset. Perhaps the removal of too many bass by anglers has given the panfish an edge in devouring the juvenile bass before they can mature. Trash fish, such as carp and dogfish (bowfins), also contribute to the decline in the number of bass.

You might be able to help by removing as many trash fish as possible (if they are present) or by removing a large number of panfish. If this fails, you should consult the state fishery-management personnel and have them examine the lake to diagnose its problem. They may conduct netting operations to preserve the ecology of the lake. Then the introduction of fingerling bass could soon bring the lake back to normal.

Is electronic fish-finding gear really necessary to locate bass in deep water?

If not absolutely necessary, it certainly helps a lot and saves time spent hunting for bass by blind trolling. Fish-finders come in assorted sizes, but they all measure the water depth. Some of the recorder models will pinpoint bass on a chart— giving you a positive location.

In Florida there's no closed season on bass, since they spawn practically every month of the year. I like to go after those big males standing guard over their nests, but I have poor luck with commotion plugs and live bait. Do you have any suggestions?

Using the right bait at the right time is one of the big tricks in catching bass, especially when they are finicky while "bed-tending." During the spawning season, a bullhead minnow (a true scavenger) is the prime enemy of bass. A bass guarding his nest has all he can do to keep the minnows and other intruders from gulping all his eggs. When he strikes at a bullhead, he strikes for keeps. So there's your best bait—

a live, struggling bullhead minnow, 3 to 6 inches long, with a hook impaled in its back just forward of the dorsal fin.

What is a spotted bass? (It is also called a Kentucky spotted bass.)

Although it has some of the characteristics of both the small-mouth and the largemouth bass, this hybrid bass is identified as a distinct species. Its average weight is less than that of either the smallmouth or the largemouth. Spotted bass seldom weigh more than 5 pounds.

The color characteristics are similar to those of the large-mouth, but the markings are diamond-shaped and more pronounced.

Spotted bass are found in the Ohio-Mississippi drainage from Illinois and Ohio south to the Gulf states, into western Florida, and west to Texas, Oklahoma, and Kansas.

What is the best way to cook bass? Perhaps I have the wrong recipe, because they always seem to have a "muddy" flavor.

Bass, especially the lunkers, often have a "muddy" taste, but most of this objectionable flavor is removed when the bass is skinned and filleted—leaving the mild white flesh.

A variety of cooking methods can be applied to bass fillets. You can broil, bake, or pan-fry them. However, rolling them in cornmeal and frying them in deep fat seems to be the favorite method of most fish lovers.

Can you tell me if there are any schools that actually teach freshwater fishing? I don't mean casting schools. I'm interested specifically in _bass_ fishing.

You're in luck! The Garcia Bass Fishing School runs a 3-day session on Lake Powell, Colorado. The tuition is $260 per person and includes personalized instruction with guides, equipment, license, lodging, and meals. The curriculum covers bass biology, electronic gear, reading structures, techniques, etc.

For complete details, write
   Garcia Bass Fishing School
   650 S. Lipan
   Denver, Colo. 80223

2

The Pikes

NORTHERN PIKE

How big do northern pike get, and what is the rod-and-reel record?

Sixty-pounders have been caught occasionally in commercial nets, but the rod-and-reel record is a 46-pounder caught in the Sacandaga Reservoir, New York, in 1940.

Why are the northern pike caught near the Arctic Circle much smaller than those caught farther south?

Environmental and frequent climatic changes near the edge of the pike's range can slow their growth. A meager or inconsistent food supply also retards a fish's growth.

What is the growth rate of northern pike?

The rate of growth depends directly upon habitat and latitude. Under almost ideal conditions which might exist somewhere near the border of the United States and Canada, northerns grow at a rapid rate. Some specimens under study grew 17.6 inches in 171 days. Some yearlings in Michigan averaged 14.7 inches. A reservoir in Pennsylvania produced a pike that grew to 39.5 inches in 5 summers.

Northerns from Great Bear Lake, which lies on the Arctic Circle in Canada, took 7 years to reach 20 inches and 12 years to reach 30 inches. On the other hand, Minnesota proudly boasts of pike that grow from 12 to 18 inches at the end of the first year. If weight is a measure of distinction, perhaps we should call them "southerns."

Is it true that pike are able to eat fish their own size?

The pike family are notorious cannibals which are physiologically equipped to swallow portions as big as they are—including their own kin!

Are there any subspecies of northern pike?

Since northerns are circumpolar in their distribution, there are two subspecies in eastern Siberia. With one, there is the possibility that it may reach into Alaska and Canada. The other Siberian subspecies is spotted and resembles the muskellunge.

Another subspecies, called the silver pike, is frequently encountered in Minnesota, Canada, and Sweden and is distinguished from the northern pike by its markings and color. It is a mutation that seldom exceeds 10 pounds, but in fighting characteristics it is similar to others of the pike family.

In what water temperatures are northerns most comfortable while still retaining their keen appetites?

Scientific studies show that pike prefer a temperature range from 50 to 70 degrees F.

What kind of disposition do pike have, and what are their spawning habits?

Pike are savage, voracious eaters that attack any other fish, reptile, or small mammal. They're able to consume about one-fifth of their weight in a day. Since their diet is composed mainly of fish, they should never be transplanted into lakes that contain a lot of smaller and less savage species.

Northerns are solitary fish; they seldom school and like to conceal themselves among sunken treetops (plentiful in impoundments) or lurk among underwater weed beds and lily pads.

During their spawning season (early spring to June) pike migrate into the shallows, preferring soft muddy bottoms and weedy marshes. There's no ceremony to the spawning rites— eggs are dropped and fertilized and the parents split! The eggs are given no attention and are left to survive or perish.

During the summer months, when pike and muskie fishing falls off, resort operators and guides always have excuses to offer. One is that "the fish are shedding their teeth and their gums are sore." What do you say?

Members of the pike family *do* lose a tooth or two now and then in the course of feeding, but the teeth are soon replaced. This replacement process does not interfere with the fish's eating habits.

There could be any number of reasons for poor fishing. Unsupervised stocking and poor management create an imbalance in the species and an overpopulation of trash fish. The sudden abundance of natural food, such as a population explosion of small fish, can reduce a pike's appetite.

Water temperature too will put the fish down. If the water is too warm for comfort and food supply, they will head for the deeper zone where it is more difficult for the angler to find them. If the pike can't find cooler temperatures, then they stay in shallow water and sulk. And sulk they do, since warm water quickly induces sluggishness.

Then when *is* the best time to fish for northerns?

Spring, fall, and winter ice fishing. But northerns *can* be caught during the hot summer months; you just have to work harder at it. Hunt for them. Avoid the hot afternoons, and fish only in the early-morning and evening hours.

What kinds of artificial lures are best?

Northerns are real plug splinterers and spoon twisters! Most plug patterns will catch pike if good, erratic action is given to them. Jointed plugs are favorites—both the deep and surface-swimming models. Bucktail and wobbling spoons slow-trolled have also proved themselves through the years.

I don't want to use a gaff hook or similar equipment on fish such as pike and muskies for fear of injuring them. I prefer to release most of my fish, but I find that a landing net is awkward and not large enough in some cases. Is there any other method I can employ to land fish and release them without harm?

If you grasp a pike or muskie firmly over the head with your hand, applying enough pressure on the gill covers to lift the fish from the water, it will become paralyzed momentarily—giving you time to remove your hooks. It's a tricky business and *could* be dangerous unless you make a direct, forceful grab and hang on without juggling. Most pros are able to do this without receiving a scratch.

If you think that your hand is too small, better not chance it. Use a gaff hook. A gaff can be inserted into the mouth and pulled through the tip of the lower jaw without any harmful effect. To be safe, always use a long-shank hook remover. The new models have a pistol grip and work very well.

What are the feeding habits of northern pike?

Northerns possess keen eyesight and are primarily daytime feeders. They prey upon everything that moves. The viciousness of their attacks makes them a favorite sport fish of anglers. Northerns are especially fond of smaller fishes such as suckers, minnows, and perch. However, field mice, ducklings, frogs, and birds are not excluded from their diets.

Northern pike usually inhabit weed beds during their feeding periods, but when their appetites have been satisfied they head for deeper water outside. Large northerns may feed well into the night, but the small ones usually get their fill during the day.

How do I go about finding a good spot to ice-fish for pike?

Pike usually inhabit water 4 to 8 feet deep adjacent to weed beds. Since you can't see through the ice, the only way to find good locations is by trial and error. Begin where you know a weedy bottom exists, spacing your tip-ups about 50 feet apart. Try at least four or five holes, and if you don't have any luck within a half hour, move elsewhere. Keep a record of your locations, trying closer to shore or farther out in the lake, shifting them back and forth parallel to the shoreline until you find a productive area.

How large should I make the holes, what is the best bait, and what size hook should I use?

Using a spud or ice chisel, cut your holes at least 18 inches in diameter. The larger the better, so that they won't freeze over so quickly and there is less chance of losing a fish as you bring it through.

Lively shiners or minnows, 2 to 3 inches long, are the best bait. Larger, if you suspect bigger fish. A size 2 or 3 hook is preferred. Lip-hooking the shiners seems to catch more pike than hooking the bait through the back just forward of the dorsal fin.

MUSKELLUNGE

How large do muskellunge get, and what is the present world's rod-and-reel record?

Muskies weighing up to 90 pounds have been caught infrequently by unorthodox methods.

The existing rod-and-reel record is 69 pounds 15 ounces. The beauty was caught in the St. Lawrence River, New York, in 1957.

How can you distinguish between the muskellunge and the northern pike, especially if they're equal in size and weight?

The lower half of the gill cover and cheek of the muskellunge does not have any scales. The species can also be recognized by its markings. The adult northern pike always has light elongated spots on its sides, while the muskellunge may exhibit dark spots, markings that are bar-shaped, or no markings at all.

The number of sensory pores located on the lower jaw, or mandible of each species can identify the fish. Each side of the muskellunge's mandible contains six to nine sensory pores, while the mandible of the northern pike contains only five.

How many subspecies of muskellunge are there, and what is their range?

There are three subspecies. The Ohio, or Chautauqua, muskellunge is found in Lake Chautauqua and in the Ohio River drainage.

The Great Lakes muskellunge inhabits the waters of the Great Lakes Basin.

The northern, or tiger, muskellunge is found in the Upper Peninsula of Michigan, Wisconsin, Minnesota, and the tributary waters of Hudson Bay in Canada.

New procedures in artificial propagation extend these ranges considerably.

Why aren't muskies and northerns found in the same lake?

There are some instances where muskies are found in the waters inhabited by northerns, usually the larger lakes of Upper Michigan, Wisconsin, Minnesota, and Canada. The two species have the same feeding habits, being fish eaters primarily, but they have little rapport with each other, particularly in smaller lakes.

Muskies spawn two to four weeks after northerns. If the young of both species are present, the northerns will be larger and are likely to feed on the muskies. The slower-maturing muskies reach spawning age at 5 years, 1 to 3 years after the northerns.

Do the species ever crossbreed?

Yes, they do, and the results are spectacular. If and when northern pike and muskies manage to live together during the spawning season, their spawn will sometimes cross-fertilize and produce the boldly striped tiger muskellunge.

In Wisconsin, this crossbreeding is *not* a biological accident. Hybridization is practiced in the hatcheries with successful results.

What are the spawning habits of the muskellunge?

Muskies like the soft and muddy bottoms full of detritus and weeds for spawning purposes. They prefer shallow water, and the eggs are scattered promiscuously over a wide area without parental care. Spawning takes place in the spring, usually in April or May when temperatures are at least 50 degrees or warmer.

A 30- to 40-pound female can deposit as many as 300,000 eggs in a single season. Depending upon the water temperature, the eggs will hatch in 10 to 15 days. The young start foraging for themselves as soon as their yolk sacs are absorbed.

Are muskies gregarious? What are their feeding habits?

No, they are not gregarious. Except for the first year or two, when they school and travel together, muskies are solitary fish. As they become adults, the schools thin out and each will choose his own territory. They are known to select one small area and remain there for several years. Although they may leave their territories during breeding periods, they always return, year after year, to their favorite haunts.

They like to lie in concealed spots—hiding among weeds and boulders or lurking under submerged vegetation and logs—waiting patiently for their prey to appear. Woe be to intruders, such as small fish, ducks, birds, mice, small beaver, and other small fur-bearing animals! Like cats, muskies stalk and ambush their prey and, after seizing it in their mouths, will hold it for a long time before eating it.

Unlike most other fish, muskies are extremely temperamental and suspicious. They often refuse the baits or lures that an angler offers. For some anglers, fishing for muskies is a frustrating and discouraging experience, while other anglers find muskie fishing a supreme challenge.

How big does the muskie get, and what is its rate of growth?

Like its close relative the northern pike, the muskie is one

of the fastest-growing species among the freshwater fishes.
The muskie becomes much larger than the northern pike,
reaching a length of 6 feet and attaining an average weight of
15 to 30 pounds. Occasionally anglers have caught muskies
weighing 50 to 60 pounds, and 80- and 90-pounders have been
caught in nets set by conservation departments during the
spawning season.

A female muskie grows faster than a male and can measure
as much as 6 inches longer in her fifth year. An average muskie
from northern waters will reach 30 inches in length in its
fourth or fifth year, depending upon food availability.

The age of a muskie is determined from the scales and rings
found in its vertebral discs. A 70-pound giant was found to be
30 years old! Muskies grow more rapidly during their first
three years, but then the growth rate decreases until, about
the twelfth year, it averages about 1 inch per year. Growth is
faster during the early summer and early fall when temperatures are favorable.

**When I'm after big muskies I like to use a large live sucker or
redhorse for bait. But I'm not sure how long to let a fish have
the bait before I strike him. Is there any special timing or
technique involved?**

The muskellunge is not what I would call a voracious feeder
when he grabs a large bait. He's pretty cautious and wary,
especially when he feels a slight resistance caused by a tight
line or when his jaws clamp down on the bait's harness.

After a muskie takes a large bait, forget about the old rule of
giving him 5 to 10 minutes before striking. There's no set time
or pattern to his notions. It all depends on several factors, such
as how great his appetite is, how large he is compared with
his bait, and how much caution he exercises. A muskie always
makes a short run with a large bait in his mouth and then
pauses (for the above reasons) before or while he turns it
around to swallow it headfirst. The time involved varies, and
no attempt should be made to outguess him. When he makes
his second run it's almost certain that he has swallowed the
bait, and *only then* do you set the hook.

Where are some of the hot spots to fish for muskellunge?

There's good water up and down the St. Lawrence River in New York. Some stretches from Waddington to Ogdensburg and upriver as far as Chippewa Bay near Hammond have consistently produced muskies in the 40-pound class. Manitou Lake, Lake of the Woods, and Vermilion Lake in Ontario, Canada, have also given anglers top action. The Leech Lake and Red Lake districts in Minnesota are popular too.

What artificial lures do you recommend for catching muskies?

The Pikie-Minnow plugs are old standbys. Get the different models to suit your water conditions (shallow, deep, trolling, or casting). Cisco Kids and Swimming Whizz plugs are very popular. Spoons such as Dardevle, Swim Zag, Marathon Rattle, and Williams Wabler are musts if conditions are likely.

The muskie tackle box isn't complete without its assorted bucktails. These are used on the days when nothing else seems to work. Popular models contain lead weights hidden near the swivel snaps so that they won't foul. Slim Jim, Marathon Musky Hawk, and Micky Finn are the favorites.

What kind of leaders should I use?

Use wire leaders with barrel swivels and snaps for trolling and casting. A muskie's sharp teeth and gill covers can cut lines in no time. If you're trolling, a leader at least 36 inches long should be used to prevent line breakage. Sometimes, after a muskie is hooked, he'll roll up in the leader and snap it. For casting you'll have to use a shorter length of leader. An 18- or 24-inch (whichever is more comfortable for distance casting) braided steel wire is best.

When a muskie strikes an artificial lure, how and when do I set the hooks?

You'd better strike back harder than he does! And your hooks had better be sharp, since in many cases they have to be driven into bone and tough gristle. You've got to be alert and prepared to strike fast. Keep your rod down and the tip pointed at your lure in the water so that you can make a full, effective swing when you strike your fish.

What is the best way to land a big muskie safely if a net is too small?

Be ready for the big one at all times. This means carrying a gaff. Gaff him through the jaw (inside out) and snatch him swiftly into the boat.

Gaffing a heavy fish in the jaw gives you more leverage while holding his head up, and he's less likely to flip off the gaff. If you think your fish is too big or too heavy to lift from the water, then you should crack him on the cranium with a lead billy club (the saltwater type, used for billfish) while you have the gaff in his mouth and he's still on top of the water.

Is spinning tackle practical for catching muskies?

Yes, if you're happy with hooking only small ones and releasing them because they are of illegal size. In some states, 28 to 30 inches is the minimum length for keepers.

No, if you want to hold on to your muskies, especially the big ones. (Releasing them after landing is more fun!) You should use a bait-casting rod about 6 feet long with plenty of backbone to cast or troll heavy artificials and to set the hooks firmly into that tough mouth.

Your best line is 20- to 30-pound-test Dacron. It doesn't stretch like monofilament or twist like nylon and is good for those strikes that require an instant hookup.

Use the best casting reels you can afford. Throwing heavy baits all day is hard on any reel, so buying top quality pays off.

I'd like to try fishing for muskies, but I don't know much about them except what I've read. Should I hire a guide for my first trip?

Yes, emphatically! Muskies are big, tough, tricky, and hard to find. A knowledge of their haunts in any given lake is well worth the guide's fee. In addition, you'll learn much more: the rate of speed in retrieving and trolling, the choice of lures for different situations, and proper techniques in searching, hooking, and landing.

PICKEREL

How many species of pickerel are there, and what is the difference between them and the northern pike?

There are three species of pickerel: the grass pike, or little pickerel; the eastern chain pickerel; and the barred pickerel. The grass pike and the barred pickerel rarely measure over 12 inches. The eastern chain pickerel averages 3 pounds, but 10- or 12-pounders are frequently caught.

The northern pike resembles the pickerels, but its gill covers are only half scaled, while the gill covers of the pickerels are fully scaled. This is about the only simple way to distinguish between these species when they are small. However, the northern pike grows rapidly and soon attains a weight of 15 pounds, with 20- and 25-pounders prevalent.

What did the world's rod-and-reel record pickerel weigh?

The chain pickerel weighed 9 pounds 6 ounces and was caught in Homersville, Georgia, in 1961.

What position does the pickerel hold in the sport-fishing community?

Because of their limited size and distribution, pickerel do not achieve the fame that their celebrated cousins do. However, they are just as gamy, pound for pound, and can be caught on the same tackle and with the same techniques as those used on northerns and muskies. Of course, you should use smaller lures and lighter gear. Pickerel can be great sport on a fly rod, with multicolored streamers, frog bugs, and poppers.

3

The Perches

WALLEYE

To what family does the walleye belong? Who are his relatives?

Walleyes are the largest species in the perch family. Saugers and yellow perch are also members of the family.

How much did the largest walleye caught on rod and reel weigh?

A 25-pounder is the world's record, caught in Old Hickory Lake, Tennessee in 1960.

What kind of water and bottom do walleyes like?

During the summer months, walleyes are found in deep-water lakes more often than in shallow rivers. They prefer clear water with temperatures of 60 degrees F. or less, and lakes with gravel or sandy bottoms. Walleyes are also found in man-made reservoirs as long as a normal food chain exists to ensure their propagation.

In the spring and fall, when water temperatures are cooler, they will be found in shallower water.

What natural foods do walleyes eat?

Walleyes are piscivorous, which means that their diet is made up mostly of fish. They are very fast and can be voracious feeders when confronted with their own species (smaller versions) or relatives (perch) and think nothing of chasing a bass half their size.

These lively mudminnows are excellent natural bait for walleyes—whether you're still-fishing, drifting with a Lindy Rig, or slow-trolling deep with a June Bug spinner. (HAL SCHARP)

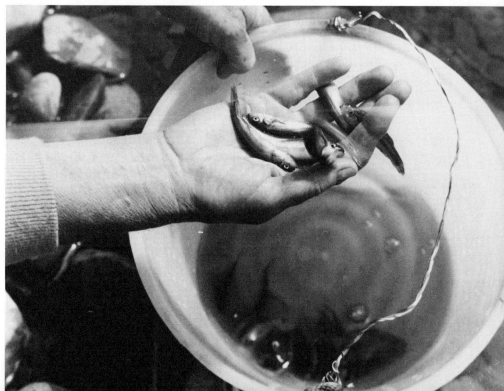

What is the growth rate of the walleye?

Under normal conditions, such as water fertility and a favorable climate, walleyes measure 12 to 15 inches at the end of the second year. In their third year, when they are 18 to 20 inches in length, they are able to spawn. Southern walleyes grow larger than the northern variety, but the northern midgets enjoy a much longer life-span.

What is a good way to catch walleyes?

Although walleyes are cousins to the perch, their feeding habits and personalities are completely different. Walleyes are essentially deep-water fish and are usually found lurking about the edges of bars and rock ledges during the day. They forage in shallow water only during the early-morning and evening hours.

Live bait is best, since they feed largely upon other fish. They're voracious feeders that will attack practically any small live bait, but they show a definite preference for mudminnows.

Artificial lures that simulate small baitfish or minnows are best, but only the deep underwater models should be used, because walleyes seldom take a surface bait. Wobbler plugs, spoons, and streamer bucktails with spinners are excellent lures. Also, a June Bug spinner trailing a mudminnow in harness is a real killer for slow-trolling deep over ledges and rocky bottoms.

How did the walleye acquire its name?

Obviously, it has something to do with its eyes. If you look at them, you will notice a milky-white, glassy cast that is like a blank wall.

What other names are given to the walleye?

Glasseye, jack salmon, pike perch, walleyed pike, blue fish, doré, and many other regional names.

Under what weather conditions will walleyes be found hungry and cooperative?

On cool days and during stormy weather, walleyes will be found feeding in the shallows during the early-morning and afternoon hours. They can be found on the windward side of islands and bars on windy days. Always fish the downwind shore areas.

It has been noted that walleyes feed extremely well during a full moon and that the best time to catch the extra-large lunkers is during the brightest phase of the moon from 10 P.M. to 2 A.M.

What is a good artificial lure to use in deep-trolling for walleyes?

Most deep-running plugs, patterned after fish shapes and colors, will catch walleyes. Flatfishes have been popular for many years.

How should this lure be worked to be most effective?

To rig a weighted floating plug you simply fasten a keel sinker (weighted to suit the depth required to reach the bottom) at the junction where your line is attached to your leader (which should be at least 24 inches long). This rig will let you bounce your sinker along the bottom while your floating plug swims clear at the proper depth. You can cast from shore into deep depressions at the base of river dams or slow-troll from a boat.

SAUGER

In what way does the sauger resemble the walleye?

In many respects, the sauger's appearance, behavior, food habits, and habitat are nearly identical to those of the walleye. They even taste the same.

The sauger, however, likes plenty of room—preferring large lakes over the smaller bodies of water that walleyes seem to tolerate well.

The only outstanding dissimilarity is the sauger's size. Although the two fishes seem identical, their sizes are highly disproportionate—so much so that an adult sauger can be mistaken for a baby walleye.

What is the world's rod-and-reel record for saugers?

An 8-pound-12-ounce sauger was caught in Lake Sakakowea, North Dakota, in 1971. Commercial netters often produce 10-pounders.

By what other names is the sauger known?

A favorite name in many regions is sand pike. It is also known as jack fish, jack salmon, river pike, and spotfin pike.

How do the sauger's fighting qualities stack up against the walleye's?

A little on the weak side. The sauger is not quite as vigorous in the tug-o'-war department as the walleye—who, incidentally, does not rank with the best. But compared with many other fishes, saugers *do* make a good showing in resisting capture.

Why don't saugers thrive in small bodies of water or in rivers?

Biologists still haven't been able to offer any explanation. This is a subject of continuous research, since the sauger is becoming an important food fish and an ideal supplement in the stocking programs of sport fisheries.

Saugers seem to insist upon migrating great distances, which just contributes to the mystery.

Where are saugers found?

They are scattered in the central states and in the largest lakes of the northern states and southern Canada. The tailwaters of dams at the end of large impoundments will contain heavy concentrations, especially during late-fall and early-winter seasonal runs.

What is the growth rate of the sauger?

Southern saugers grow 6 to 8 inches in each of their first two years and about 1½ inches each year thereafter, making a 3-year-old sauger 14 to 18 inches long. They can reach 30 inches toward the end of their life-span.

Like walleyes, saugers in the northern climates grow much more slowly but live longer.

YELLOW PERCH

How big do yellow perch get, and what is their growth rate?

Yellow perch weighing 6 pounds have been caught by unorthodox methods such as the trotline-trolley technique (commonly used along Chicago's lakefront).

Their growth rate depends upon the fertility of the water

and the geographical location, but they average 3 inches the first year, 3 inches the second year, 2 inches the third, and 1 inch each year thereafter.

What is the world's rod-and-reel record?

According to the *Field & Stream* magazine records, the largest yellow perch weighed 4 pounds 3½ ounces and was caught in Bordentown, New Jersey.

What position do yellow perch hold among rod-and-reel game fishes?

Not very prominent. They are strictly a fly-rod and cane-pole fish—but they provide fast spirited action and excellent table fare. They could be classed as a gamy panfish.

By what other names are yellow perch known?

Nicknames such as convict perch and ring perch are carelessly bestowed, while other regional names, such as raccoon perch and striped perch, are given sincerely in a particular locale. Jumbo is a popular name along the shores of the Great Lakes if the perch weigh 1 pound or more.

What does a yellow perch's diet consist of?

Perch are not finicky eaters. A hungry one will grab at any natural bait, including the spawn of whitefish. They're predaceous and capable of wiping out the spawn or young of other important fishes in lakes and ponds, if their introduction is managed carelessly.

Fish eggs, small minnows, insects, crayfish, and other aquatic crustaceans make up the rest of their diet.

What bait is best and least likely to be nibbled off before the hook can be set?

Bits of crabmeat called "peelers," small minnows, and the old standby—worms—all used on a size 6 hook.

How about artificials using a fly rod?

Streamer flies resembling the local minnows and wet flies matched with the insect of the season are good lures. Also, small spinners will make good catches.

4

The Panfishes

I want to create a pond on my property, where I have a natural water supply from several marsh springs. I'd like to stock only panfish such as crappies, bluegills, and sunfish. What's the best way to go about this, and what kind of food should I use?

Before you begin, it would be wise to consult your local warden and the state fish-and-game commission for advice. Since private ponds are becoming more popular, state biologists will be glad to help you stock your pond and will give you all the necessary information about food to make your pond a successful venture.

You'll probably be forced to introduce some largemouth bass to control the panfish population. Otherwise, a population explosion among the panfish could create a shortage of food which will stunt their growth.

How should a worm be hooked for still-fishing for panfish?

Run the hook through the worm three or four times and

THE PANFISHES

A worm threaded on a hook is a universal favorite for panfish. If it still doesn't work, better try giving it "one for good luck"! (PENNSYLVANIA FISH COMMISSION)

embed the point and barb in the head. If nibblers are stealing the worms, use only a small piece, thread it on the hook, and bury the point and barb completely.

If the panfish are running big and sassy, don't be afraid to thread two or more worms on a single hook.

I often hear anglers say that the fish are "bedding." What does that mean?

"Bedding" usually refers to the spawning of panfish such as crappies, redear sunfish, and bluegills. As a rule, this takes place in the spring when the shallow water begins to warm to the proper temperature for hatching. Larger fish such as bass and trout that also spawn in the shallows are often referred to as "bedding fish."

BLUEGILL

What are some of the regional names of the bluegill?

In the southeastern states, bluegills are known as bream (or "brim" in the deep South!). In other locales, they are called copperbellies, blue sunfish, and perch.

What is the rod-and-reel record for bluegills?

A 4-pound-12-ounce bluegill was caught in Ketona Lake, Alabama, in 1950.

What is their distribution?

At one time, bluegills had a limited distribution ranging from Lake Champlain in the east to the Great Lakes region, south to Georgia, and west to Arkansas. Because of their ability to adapt to any reasonable aquatic community, they are presently thriving very well in most ponds and lakes throughout the United States.

What is their angling value?

Bluegills are spunky little beggars that offer great sport on superlight tackle. They'll take practically any kind of natural bait and relish all sorts of artificial flies.

In what kind of habitat do bluegills thrive best?

Small bluegills feel safe and comfortable in weedy areas that provide enough cover to hide them from predators such as pike and bass and still contain sufficient aquatic food.

Larger bluegills will venture into deeper and less secluded water during the daytime, but return to the shallow weed beds to feed at dawn and in the evening.

REDEAR SUNFISH

What is the range and distribution of the redear sunfish?

Redears are limited to the southern United States from Indiana to Florida and west to New Mexico.

By what other names are redear sunfish called?

Yellow bream, stumpknocker, and shellcracker. "Shellcrackers" (a Florida alias) possess well-developed grinding teeth in their throats which give them the ability to crush snails (a major part of their diet).

Is there a record of the largest redear sunfish caught on rod and reel?

A 4-pound-8-ounce monster was caught at Chase City, Virginia, in 1970.

What is their position in the angling fraternity?

First of all, they are an excellent-tasting panfish. As far as action is concerned, they don't respond well to artificial flies—but present a worm or a shrimp on a No. 6 hook and you'll get a jolt!

What kind of surroundings do redears prefer?

Redears like quiet water, but unlike other panfish, they have no special preference for vegetation or weedy areas. They'd rather congregate around tree stumps (the origin of the nickname "stumpknocker"), roots, and logs lying at the bottom of deep water.

ROCK BASS

How big do rock bass get?

Not very big in size, but they are big in game qualities. The world's record caught by rod and reel was 3 pounds and was taken from the York River, Ontario, Canada, in 1974.

What kind of feeders are they, and will they take a fly?

Rock bass are voracious feeders that will pounce on any natural bait, artificial flies, or small popping bugs.

What other names do they have?

Depending upon their geographical location, you can call them black perch, goggle-eye, redeye, and rock sunfish.

What kind of habitat do they prefer?

They are strict rocky-bottom dwellers, and they feed exclusively upon the aquatic insects and crustaceans that inhabit their environment. They like the cool waters of clear streams that contain gravel or boulders.

WARMOUTH

Where does the warmouth like to lurk?

Warmouths are one of the few species that can tolerate turbid water. They prefer dense weeds and soft muddy bottoms.

How large do they get?

A 1-pounder is a whopper! The largest on record caught with rod and reel strained the scales at 2 pounds even. The historic battle took place in Sylvania, Georgia, in 1974.

What are they like as a sport fish?

Ounce for ounce, they're tough when you use extra-light tackle. Warmouths can be caught on any small natural bait such as grubs, aquatic insect larvae, and worms. They even take small flies such as gnats, bees, etc.

WHITE BASS

How does the white bass stack up against the largemouth and smallmouth bass?

It leaves a lot to be desired! But, like panfish, on extremely light tackle, it gives a credible account of itself. Fishery commissions throughout the United States find it a valuable supplement to their game-fish restocking programs.

What is the largest on the record books taken by rod and reel?

A 5-pound-5-ounce white bass caught on Ferguson Lake, California, in 1972.

How do the habits and behavior of white bass compare with those of the largemouth and smallmouth bass?

White bass inhabit large, deep lakes or streams. They like plenty of room, seldom ascend smaller streams or creeks, and are indifferent to the secretive hiding places like lily pads, weeds, stumps, or submerged treetops. Gregarious by nature, they school by the hundreds and are unpredictable and easily frightened by the slightest sound or movement.

What kinds of artificial lures are best for white bass?

Since these are small fish, averaging ¾ to 1½ pounds, lures should never be over 2 inches long. The size of the lure should match the shad hatch the bass are feeding on. Spoons, bucktails, yellow or white marabou, and white and shad-scale plugs are all effective.

For surface fishing, the Mirrolure, Shad-Roe, Bayou Boogie, Silly Billy, Spot-Tail, and Mepps Spinners are all killers.

For deep-trolling, use a diving plug rigged with a feather popping bug trailing 18 inches in the rear.

Is it true that the white bass is the only *true* freshwater bass in the whole clan of basses, while the others are members of the sunfish family?

Yes. The white bass is a deviant from the famous saltwater striped bass. Many years ago, striped bass entered freshwater rivers to spawn. Eventually, some of the species became land-locked, found their way into other tributaries, and adapted successfully to their environment, although their size diminished markedly from that of their ancestors.

What is the range of white bass?

White bass are found throughout the Great Lakes region, in areas between the Alleghenies and the Mississippi, on down through the South, and in many western states.

They thrive very well in reservoirs, where their successful propagation continues to make them a popular fish.

CRAPPIE

How many species of crappie are there?.

There are two distinct species—the black crappie and the white crappie.

By what other names are they known?

The black crappie is known as calico bass, speckled perch, and strawberry bass.

Regional names of the white crappie are papermouth, white perch, bride perch, bachelor, and lamplighter.

Do the two species share the same environment?

No. The black crappie prefers less turbid water and more vegetation than the white. It's found chiefly in the cooler waters of clear lakes and streams containing rocks and gravel.

The white crappie is found mostly in mid-South river systems, ponds, bayous, and sloughs. It is fond of warm water, muddy bottoms, and slightly alkaline water.

Which species is more abundant?

The white crappie, which has a slightly greater range and distribution.

When are crappies found in great abundance?

The largest population is in the spring of the year prior to spawning.

How long do crappies live, and what are their mannerisms?

Both species have a short life-span, ranging from 4 to 6 years. They're gregarious by nature, so they school a lot.

What are the world's rod-and-reel records for these species?

In 1957, a black crappie was caught in the Santee-Cooper Reservoir, South Carolina, that weighed an even 5 pounds. A 5-pound-3-ounce white crappie was caught at the Enid Dam, Mississippi, in 1957.

What is the most popular method for catching crappies?

Most anglers prefer minnow fishing with a fly rod or cane pole. A popular technique is to hook lively minnows through the eye sockets, using a light-wire Aberdeen hook, and let the crappie make a short run before setting the hook.

Fly-rod enthusiasts have excellent success with small $\frac{1}{16}$- to $\frac{1}{32}$-ounce bucktail jigs (white pattern) rigged in tandem, 18 inches apart. These will usually produce immediate and continual action, once a school is located.

Crappies will also hit small flies or poppers at dusk, but certain patterns have to be chosen for their acceptance. Work all these lures as slowly as possible with an occasional slight twitching action.

What is the chief diet of each species?

The adult black crappie feeds on crustaceans, aquatic insects, and small fish.

The white crappie feeds mainly on small fish after it reaches maturity.

What is an effective way to find a school of crappies in open water?

Very slow deep-trolling with a small spinner and a minnow behind it. Troll just fast enough to revolve the spinner blade.

REDEYE BASS

Is the redeye bass a smallmouth black bass?

No, not really. There's a Flint River smallmouth in Georgia that closely resembles the redeye, but it is strictly a subspecies.

What is the world's record for redeyes with rod and reel?

In 1975, a 7-pound-8-ounce specimen was caught in Lazer Creek, Georgia.

Where are redeyes found?

Redeyes have a limited range and are found only in the southeastern United States.

What kind of environment do redeyes inhabit?

Upland drainage areas, small streams, and ponds. They seem to tolerate only warm water, but its clarity and bottom characteristics mean little to this species.

How does the redeye rate as a game fish?

Similar to a smallmouth bass—a terrific scrapper and a leading game panfish. Redeyes take all kinds of artificials and natural baits eagerly.

5

The Trouts

I'd like to learn some of the fine points of fly fishing for stream trout. What can you suggest that will help me get started on the right foot?

You should learn the habits of trout in their various and changing habitats. Familiarize yourself with their natural food supply. This means acquiring a knowledge of the life cycles of aquatic insects so that you can match their hatches successfully. Also, you must learn to identify and understand the movements of flying insects that are indigenous to the particular stream you're fishing.

Good, balanced fly tackle and instructions from a pro certainly mean a great deal. Practice your casting in your backyard when you're not fishing in the stream.

Read a few books written by experts on this subject. You're specializing now in a sport that offers the ultimate in fishing challenges.

Join a fishing club and exchange ideas and suggestions with other members, or locate a fishing clinic that offers casting

A basic knowledge of the habits and food preferences of fish is necessary to choose the right fly pattern. (MAINE DEPT. OF ECONOMIC DEVELOPMENT)

instruction and advice on tackle and technique. Such clinics are usually operated by tackle manufacturers, who are always glad to let you know when and where a series of clinic sessions will be held.

How long does it take for a trout's eggs to hatch?

Hatching depends entirely on water temperature. Brook trout spawn between fall and spring, depending upon the section of the country and the weather. The eggs of rainbow trout (which are spawned between January and April) will hatch in the spring. As the water becomes warmer, both species will hatch at about the same time. The period between spawning and hatching is about 7 to 8 weeks.

How many inches does a trout grow in a year?

In a very cold stream with a limited food supply, trout may measure only 3 to 5 inches when they reach one year. Moderate water temperatures and an abundance of food create ideal growing conditions. Under these circumstances, trout will measure 8 to 12 inches when they are a year old.

When fishing from the water's edge or along the banks of a river or stream, should you fish with the sun at your back or should you face into the sun?

You should fish with the sun at your back, so that the fish are less likely to see your movements. More important, you should fish from the shallows toward deeper water, regardless of the sun. If you can place yourself so that you're able to cast to deep water (fish can see you more easily if they're in the shallows) but are facing the sun, you might look for a background of trees or shrubbery to keep you from being seen.

What are "quiet holds"?

"Quiet holds" are found only in currents or swift water that contain obstructions to the flow. As the water moves over and around a boulder lying on the bottom of a fast stream, an area of slow-moving water is created surrounding the boulder. Fish often stop to rest in these calm waters.

In trout fishing, which requires greater skill in presentation, a wet or a dry fly?

Both wet- and dry-fly presentations require equal skill. Wet-fly fishing requires expertise in manipulating artificial aquatic lures to create the natural movements made by minnows, crustaceans, and insects underwater.

On the other hand, fishing with dry flies means manipulating artificial terrestrial insects on top of the water. A fly must land upon the water surface naturally and be made to simulate the movements of a struggling insect.

Is it necessary to use a weight when I'm fishing salmon eggs for trout?

Only in spots where a stream is swift and deep. Otherwise, unweighted salmon eggs appear more natural while they are drifting in the current.

What is the best way to fish a dry fly in swift water?

Obviously, since the purpose of a dry fly is to float, you must

Let your fly drift to the trout lying in deep, slow-moving current next to the riffles created by gravel bars. (COLORADO GAME, FISH & PARK DIVISION)

steer clear of fast water. Seek out the smooth runs and pools where a fly won't sink.

You should make your cast upstream, stripping the line as the fly returns to you but only fast enough to take up the slack without pulling the fly under. When the drift is completed, proceed at once to make your next cast.

During the middle of the summer when the streams are low, it's hard to get a rise from trout with artificial flies. Yet there are always a few anglers who manage to get their limits. What's the secret of their success?

Better spend more time watching those pros who don't find it beneath their dignity to resort to live bait. At this time of year, trout are waiting for landborne insects, such as beetles and "hoppers," to satisfy their appetites.

Use a large butterfly net to capture a bunch of insects. Catch enough to chum the trout. Toss them out onto the water one at a time so that they drift into a possible trout lair. Watch closely. If a trout begins to rise to the real thing, stop the chum and give him the imitation.

Why is it that large trout are seldom seen near the surface and are more difficult to catch with dry flies than smaller trout?

Larger trout tend to feed on or near the bottom and seldom rise for a small fly. Big trout will always favor a minnow, and that is why they can be caught with more success on streamer flies and bucktails than on the smaller dry flies or other surface lures.

How should I hook a worm when I'm fishing for trout in a stream?

Since there is usually a current running, the worm must appear natural—that is, allowed to drift with the current. It should be hooked only once, through the girdle, or collar. This leaves both ends free to wiggle and drift. Because the current does the work, there should be no drag on the line. This creates the appearance of a worm bouncing along with the current. It goes slowly through the pools and quickly through the shallows or riffles.

Which is the most effective fly to use in fishing for trout?

There is no good all-around fly that will catch trout at all times. You should watch what trout are doing. If they're rising to flies, then you use a dry fly; if not, then use a wet fly or nymph.

Since aquatic insects in their larval stage constitute the bulk of the trout's natural food, nymphs might be your best bet.

If a hatch of insects is taking place or just starting, what would be a fast and effective way to find out what flies trout are taking?

To simulate the changing phases of the hatch from a stream-bed nymph to the dun or adult fly (already developed and flying), use a nymph, a wet fly, and a dry fly—all three of the same pattern at the same time. A very natural combination is presented if you tie the nymph to the tippet so that it will drift at the leader end much deeper than the wet fly, which you tie to a dropper (auxiliary line to the leader). The wet fly should be located only a few inches below the floating dry fly.

You might do well to check state laws on the legal aspects of using three flies. If only two are allowed, use the nymph/dry-fly combination.

What actually takes place when a "hatch" is going on?

Many subaquatic insects such as nymphs rise to the surface to complete the metamorphosis into duns or adult flies.

What does the expression "fish are bulging" mean?

A kind of underwater rise by a fish which, with a sudden turn of its tail while chasing nymphs in shallow water, creates a "bulge" on the water's surface. Sometimes a torpedolike wave follows the bulge.

Then what is "humping"?

Fish are "humping" when both the head and tail of the fish create a variation of the bulge on the surface of the water. A hump occurs while fish are feeding on nymphs rising to the surface.

What is meant by "smutting"?

Fish are "smutting" when they are feeding on small midges close to the water surface.

BROWN TROUT

What are some of the other names given to the brown trout?

German brown, brownie, and Loch Leven trout.

How big do brown trout get, and what is the world's rod-and-reel record?

Brown trout that are caught in large streams average bigger than those caught in smaller streams. Eight- and 10-pounders are not rare.

Literature does not give any record of brown trout caught by any means other than rod and reel. *Field & Stream* magazine's world rod-and-reel records list a brown that weighed 39 pounds 8 ounces which was caught in Lock Awe, Scotland, in 1866.

What is their range and distribution?

Brown trout are distributed throughout the United States from coast to coast and from Canada down to the northern part of the Gulf states.

When were brown trout brought to the United States?

Brown trout were introduced into the United States from Europe almost 100 years ago.

Where did they come from, and where were they planted?

The German brown trout was first imported from Germany

Brown trout that have been planted in large impoundments often grow to near-record proportions. Husky "brownies" like this 23-pounder are caught trolling deep with wobbler spoons. (UTAH DIVISION OF WILDLIFE RESOURCES)

during the early part of the 19th century. Much later, during the 1880s, the Loch Leven (a subspecies of the German brown trout) was imported from Scotland and planted in the West. Since then, these two species have interbred—not by design, but successfully; and they are presently known as the brown trout—a single species.

What kind of habitat do brown trout prefer?

Although brown trout show a decided preference for cooler water, they can tolerate warm water too. They seem to be able to adapt to or resist environmental changes that may affect or harm other species. Browns are found all over the world and are favorites of fly fishermen when they are able to stalk them in the quiet pools of streams and in crevices under overhanging banks of streams and lakes. They are often found skulking in waters that contain submerged obstacles such as logs, treetops, and boulders.

What is the growth rate of brown trout?

In the right latitude and with average water fertility, brown trout will grow to 3½ inches the first year; will measure 6 inches the second, 10 inches the third, and 14 inches the fourth year; and will grow about 2 inches a year thereafter.

What are the brown trout's spawning habits?

Depending upon the location, they spawn in the fall or in the winter months. Older trout can lay as many as 3,000 eggs, while young females may lay only 500 to 1,000 eggs. When conditions and temperatures are conducive, the young will hatch the following spring. Artificially propagated trout will take about 50 days to hatch at water temperatures of 50 degrees F.

What does a brown trout feed on?

Young brown trout have a preference for flies and aquatic insect larvae. Large brown trout too will take insects, but as a brown trout becomes "braggin' size" he will look toward minnows, worms, snails, and crustaceans for a major part of his diet. Larger specimens will even engulf small birds, mice, and frogs.

How does the brown trout rank as far as fighting qualities are concerned?

The brown trout is widely acclaimed as a trophy fish. He has his own bag of tricks, and for endurance, he ranks with the best.

Why is the brown trout so hard to catch?

Of all species of trout, the brown (Loch Leven) is the most wary and unpredictable. Its cautionary instincts may have helped it to survive better than brook or rainbow trout. A brown trout will take most of the flies that attract other trout species, provided he's in the mood to feed. Otherwise, nothing under the sun can tempt him to strike.

What are some of the more popular fly patterns that catch brown trout successfully?

Light and Dark Cahills, Cream Varients, March Browns, Quill Gordons, Blue Dun Spiders, and Royal Coachmans.

What natural baits do you recommend for brown trout?

Brown trout will often take such natural baits as angleworms, hellgrammites, grasshoppers, minnows, and night crawlers.

Are there any unusual traits in the brown trout that set them apart from the other trouts?

The browns are the wariest of all the trouts. They're suspicious, tempermental, selective, and, most of the time, just downright perplexing to fishermen. It's because of these traits and their great fighting qualities that they are a genuine challenge to the patient angler.

CUTTHROAT TROUT

What is the world's rod-and-reel record for the cutthroat trout?

A 41-pounder was caught in Pyramid Lake, Nevada, in 1925.

What is the range of the cutthroat?

The cutthroat is strictly a native of the West, distributed on the coast and inland from northern Mexico to southern Alaska. It does not thrive east of the Rocky Mountains.

What are some of the regional names given to the cutthroat?

Columbia River trout, Yellowstone cutthroat, Colorado River trout, Montana black spotted trout, and Snake River cutthroat.

How did it get the name "cutthroat"?

Its common name was derived from the prominent red slash marks located on either side of the lower jaw.

Do any of the coastal species enter salt water?

Yes, some species are anadromous. That is, they are sea-run trout entering the salt water during their second or third year and returning to the river systems after one or two years.

Have any of the cutthroat species been introduced into eastern waters?

Attempts at transplanting cutthroats have all met with failure. Although cutthroats thrive well in a great range of temperatures and under varied water conditions, they don't compete well with other fish. Unsatisfactory interbreeding has made the presence of cutthroats impractical in eastern waters.

Which species of cutthroat attains the larger size?

The coastal species that have access to the ocean and migrate to sea are always larger than the inland species.

How do the game characteristics of the cutthroat compare with those of the other true trout?

Although the cutthroat is shy and sometimes discriminating in his choice of artificials, he is still considered an active game fish. However, he does not share the same game qualities as the brown or rainbow trout who jump from the water and employ all kinds of strategies to shake free of the angler's hook. Cutthroats just don't scrap as well as other trout.

In what kind of habitat are cutthroats found?

In the smaller mountain streams, cutthroats are found around boulders and rocks, in deep pools, near overhanging banks, and in riffles. In lakes, cutthroats like areas around sandy and rocky shores and above underwater ledges.

When do cutthroats spawn, and what are their habits?

Cutthroats that inhabit lakes and streams in high altitudes will spawn during the late-spring or midsummer months. Those along the coast spawn in the spring shortly after the ice has gone.

Depending upon their size, females are able to lay 3,000 to 6,000 eggs. Female cutthroats prepare the spawning bed in streams that contain a gravel bottom.

What water depths do cutthroat trout prefer?

Cutthroats are seldom found in water more than 10 feet deep, which makes them accessible to anglers fishing along the shoreline.

GOLDEN TROUT

What is the world's rod-and-reel record for the golden trout?

In 1948, Cook's Lake, Wyoming, produced an 11-pounder.

In which states is the golden trout found?

It is native only to Golden Trout Creek in the California Sierras and later was introduced into the frigid streams and lakes of Wyoming, Idaho, and Washington.

In what kind of habitat do golden trout prosper best?

Golden trout are strictly high-altitude, cold-water trout. Elevations between 6,000 and 11,000 feet are home to this fish, who prefers extremely clear water in lakes, creeks, and streams and avoids rapids or turbulent water. Like the brown trout, goldens are fond of the quiet pools and deep areas under overhanging banks. Drop-offs from ledges and rocky shores are areas especially sought in lakes.

Is it difficult to reach the natural habitat of the golden trout?

It is usually very difficult to get to them. This is one fish that makes you walk and climb after you've gone as far as possible in your car. Some remote lakes and streams can be reached by horseback; others, only by helicopter.

What will golden trout average in weight?

In small creeks and streams, golden trout will average ¾ of a pound, depending upon the fertility of the water. In lakes, they tend to grow larger at a faster rate and will average 1 to 2 pounds. When a 4- or 5-pounder is occasionally caught, it is considered a real trophy fish.

Is this species the same golden trout found in the East?

No. The golden trout of the East is an entirely different species that is native only to New Hampshire. It is actually a char and not a true trout!

What foods make up the golden trout's diet?

The principal foods of golden trout are crustaceans and terrestrial and aquatic insects. They are especially fond of midges and caddis flies.

What fly patterns and other lures are recommended to catch goldens?

Midge patterns tied on extra-light leaders. When the

goldens can be observed rising to flies, naturally dry flies should be used. Nymphs, patterned after the caddis larvae, are also popular lures. Small streamer flies and bucktails produce when the goldens are lying deep and not rising to the surface for insects.

What are the spawning habits of the golden trout?

Depending upon the water temperature and when the ice leaves, goldens begin spawning in the late spring or early summer. Spawning normally takes place in the streams and in the areas of a lake's inlet and outlet. The eggs usually hatch in 6 to 7 weeks.

RAINBOW TROUT

What are some other names for rainbow trout?

There are myriads of regional names for the rainbow such as Kamloops, Kootenay, redsides, Nelson trout, Shasta, and others.

Rainbows that inhabit the Pacific slope of the Sierras from California to Alaska have access to the sea and usually migrate. These are called steelhead trout, and they are widely acclaimed as one of the gamest freshwater fish in the world.

They enter the salt water and spend a large part of their life there, only to return to the freshwater streams to spawn.

What is the world's record for a rainbow caught by rod and reel?

A lunker was caught in 1970 at Bell Island, Alaska, that weighed 42 pounds 2 ounces.

What range and distribution do rainbows have?

Because of transplantation, rainbows are now found all over the world, wherever conditions are suitable for their existence and propagation.

Are rainbows hardy?

One of the main reasons for the successful introduction of rainbows into areas of North America, South America, and other countries of the world is their unique ability to adapt to many varied environments—habitats that most other trout species are unable to tolerate. Rainbows are rugged individuals possessed of a physiological resistance to many aquatic diseases, and they fare well in unusually warm water which other trouts find too uncomfortable.

Rainbow aficionados will attest to the fighting qualities of this acrobat, which are indicative of its strength and health.

Rainbows are excellent subjects for artificial propagation and hybridization. This in itself is a great asset to the angling fraternity, since it helps to sustain a thriving and well-organized population.

Do rainbows that inhabit lakes weigh more than those in rivers and streams?

Yes. The rule "the larger the body of water, the larger the fish" applies to rainbows and to most other trout.

How much would an average rainbow weigh in each case?

Those in small streams might only average a pound or so. Those in larger streams or large lakes would average 2 to 4 pounds. In these larger bodies of water, 6- to 10-pounders are not rare.

Those which migrate to large inland lakes, such as the Great Lakes, and to sea (the steelhead) are indeed much larger than the nonmigratory species. Many of them will average 8 to 10 pounds, while 25-pounders are frequently caught.

What position does the rainbow trout hold with the angling fraternity?

Freshwater anglers all over the world embrace the rainbow as one of the most spectacular of the trout family. The fighting qualities of rainbow trout are unsurpassed, and their endurance unchallenged. The fact that they rise readily to a fly or wallop a lure without hesitating to consider the lure's authenticity proves that they are gamy.

What are some of the rainbow's habits?

Although a good population exists in lakes, rainbows show

When you're fishing for rainbow trout in high-altitude lakes, look for outlets from mountain runoffs. These cold-water exits always provide comfort and a constant source of food for most fish. (KIEKHAEFER CORP.)

a preference for fast water. They like areas at the head of rapids or currents and the stretches of swift-flowing water rather than the lazy, winding streams or rivers which have little water movement.

Unlike some of the other trouts, rainbows are nervous fish. They can't stay put in one location for any length of time; like to move about; and in some cases, migrate extensively.

Rainbows prefer water temperatures of 70 degrees F. or cooler, but are able to tolerate 80 degrees F. for unusually long periods.

What are the spawning habits of the rainbow trout?

Since the female rainbow requires two males to service her, the spawning habits are a little different from those of other fishes. After she prepares a nest (creating a depression in the gravel on the bottom of a pool), two males wait for her and fertilize her eggs simultaneously. After this strange ritual is accomplished, the female swims upstream and proceeds to cover her eggs by washing loose gravel into the current.

When does spawning take place, and how long does it take the eggs to hatch?

Depending upon the elevation and water temperature, spawning will take place from early winter to late spring in water of 45 degrees F.

After 45 days, the eggs hatch and the young are left to fend for themselves.

What do rainbow trout feed on?

Rainbows aren't choosy. They feed upon a wide variety of natural foods. Flies, insects, worms, minnows, crustaceans, salmon eggs, and small fish make up their main diet. Large rainbows will gorge themselves on other fish and small animals such as frogs, mice, birds, and lizards.

What kinds of flies or artificial lures are best for rainbows?

No problem here. Just be at the right place at the right time. Ask the local anglers or tackle-shop owners what lures are taking rainbows at that specific time.

Rainbows are caught easily with spinning gear, so spinning lures are also effective, provided they match or imitate the natural food that the rainbows are eating. Rainbows are most often taken on minnow imitations by a fly, spinner, or bait fisherman.

STEELHEAD TROUT

What is the difference between a rainbow trout and a steelhead trout?

The steelhead is the migratory form of the rainbow. Both are scientifically classed as one, the rainbow trout. Because of their seasonal migrations into the ocean, steelhead differ in physiology, disposition, feeding and spawning habits, and fighting characteristics.

Compared with rainbows, steelheads are more elongated and streamlined. When they arrive in the streams and rivers fresh from the sea during their spawning migrations, they have a steel-blue cast and silvery sides with small, dark spots on their backs and tails. After a few weeks in fresh water, they change color and take on the appearance of the rainbows.

The steelhead is considered the greater scrapper of the two and, along with the salmon, offers the supreme challenge to any fly-rod angler.

What is the extent of a steelhead's migration?

Some outstanding examples of the distances achieved by steelhead are those that were tagged at Adok, in the Aleutian Islands, Alaska. The tags were recovered in the Columbia

River and the streams of Washington—a distance of 2,500 miles!

Will steelhead respond to the same angling techniques that we apply to the rainbow?

In a few cases, such as trolling or spinning, they will. But from the standpoint of applied fly-fishing techniques, the steelhead is a specialty fish—a different quarry altogether—one that takes a large amount of patience and experience. A working knowledge of tackle, technique, and the fish's habits are all highly important prerequisites to hooking and landing steelhead trout.

What is the best season for steelhead fishing in Washington and Oregon?

Generally speaking, as soon as the first rains come in October, the fall runs start in many of the coastal streams. However, there are many exceptions to this rule. Some runs may take place in the spring, while other rivers will have a run of steelhead in August and September. Then, in some rivers, a winter run may take place in October and last until February and March.

Although steelhead are elusive, unpredictable, and difficult to find, because of their tremendous fighting qualities they are a great challenge to fly fishermen. To catch steelhead, general or spotty information on their movements is not good enough. You have to know exactly where to run is taking place before you set out to fish for them.

How do I go about determining the seasonal movements of steelhead?

You must employ some basic strategy to locate steelhead and time your fishing trip to coincide with the run on a partic-

ular river. Since this varies greatly from river to river, you
have to do a lot of checking. Even from one year to the next,
the run of steelhead on each river varies because of weather
conditions. Try to keep your schedule flexible, so that after
you've made your inquiries about their movements, you'll still
have time to fish for them. In order to start out on the right
foot, you should constantly query outdoor writers and fly tiers
who specialize in steelheading—as well as all the local tackle
shops.

**After I've located a river where a steelhead run is going on,
how do I find the fish?**

Since steelhead move upstream rapidly, they often stop to
rest in certain spots where they can find protection from the
force of the current. These are known as "holding," or "resting," areas. You'll find steelhead along the edges of fast water
at the head or the tail of the run. Look for boulders and rocks
large enough for fish to rest or lurk behind, and check along
the sides of such obstructions. Look for outcroppings on the
banks of the river. The fish may be lying along undercut banks
or rocky ledges, or even behind logs and piled-up driftwood.
You'll find them in pools—not the deep, quiet part, but rather,
at the head or tail of the pool. Always fish from the shallow
side and cast toward the deeper side.

If the river is strange to you, it will take you some time to
learn these spots. If possible, you should study your river during the low-water periods so that you can locate depressions,
boulders, holes, and obstructions—places where a steelhead
will rest when the run is taking place at high water. Some
steelhead aficionados make their own maps of these prime
locations so that they are easier to find later. Once fish have
been taken from these spots, anglers know that they can always return and find other fish utilizing the same resting
places.

On the larger rivers, many of these spots are heavily fished
and are so crowded at times that you'll spend a lot of valuable
time running from one to another before you ever wet your

line! If you concentrate on the smaller streams and tributaries, you'll stand a better chance—provided you have an in-depth knowledge of the stream's physical characteristics. It will help a great deal if you obtain maps of these waters and become involved in some serious self-orientation.

Since I'm not good at fly fishing, is there any other way to catch steelhead?

Yes, steelhead can be caught with almost any kind of fishing outfit. Bait-casting, spinning, spin-casting, and even light surf-casting gear will all catch these fine gamesters. Of course, you must be proficient with the tackle you're using and be able to present your offering properly.

You can use your favorite outfit to drift-fish or troll for steelhead. Artificial lures, such as spoons, spinners, and plugs, are successful—provided you have located a productive area during the right time of year. The water should be clear for artificial lures to be effective.

Natural baits, such as a cluster of salmon eggs or worms, are good if they are presented properly. These will work best in high, muddy water when steelhead depend upon their sense of smell instead of their visual acuity.

I am interested specifically in the protection and promotion of trout fishing. What organization can I contact for details?

Try Trout Unlimited. It has a membership of over 15,000 who are dedicated to preserving the natural habitat of the trout—with emphasis on the sport in fishing. This organization conducts numerous research and educational programs on a national level. Contact
    Trout Unlimited
    4260 E. Evans
    Denver, Colo. 80222

6

The Chars

BROOK TROUT

What is the world's rod-and-reel record brook trout?

In 1916, a 14-pound-8-ounce brook trout was caught in the Nipigon River, Ontario, Canada.

What is one indentifying feature that distinguishes a brook trout from a true trout?

Technically, a brook trout is not a true trout at all. It is a char, which has no teeth at the rear roof of the mouth.

What other names are given to brook trout?

Speckled trout, brookie, and squaretail.

What are some of the reasons why brook trout are scarcer than other trout?

Brook trout are sensitive to water temperature, and water fertility, and have difficulty adapting to slightly polluted environments. They are also poor subjects for artificial breeding, because they lack the resistance and stamina to survive in a wilderness stream after being raised under controlled conditions in a hatchery. They are a short-lived species when compared with the longevity of other trout.

In what water temperatures do brook trout thrive best?

If they are to survive, brook trout must have cold water. This means temperatures of 65 degrees F. or less. Only rarely can 75 degrees F. be acceptable as the limit of their tolerance.

What is the range of the brook trout?

Native to northeastern North America from Georgia to the Arctic Circle, brook trout are also found wherever a suitable habitat exists in the rest of the United States. They have been transplanted to Canada, South America, and Europe with moderate success as long as the chemical and physical conditions encourage their propagation.

Where do the larger brook trout occur?

In northern Quebec, Labrador, northern Manitoba, and southern Argentina. Many of these areas contain hundreds of remote lakes and streams where brook trout averaging 4 pounds provide excellent fishing.

Since I started fly fishing, I've been having poor luck in choosing the right fly for brook trout. I'm not sure that I want to become a dry-fly purist, but I would like to improve my chances. What else can I do in addition to studying the hatch patterns on a given day?

You're on the right track. In addition, an occasional dissection of a trout's stomach can reveal many of nature's secrets. Since trout are known to be finicky in their choice of insects, a close examination of freshly ingested food will give clues to a trout's preference. Simply match the stomach contents with your fly patterns and select the fly that appears similar.

There are many instances when trout are not rising to flies. You might have to bend your principles a little if they are feeding upon other aquatic creatures such as tadpoles, frogs, crayfish, shrimp, other small crustaceans, and minnows. Then there is the worm, the tried and time-proven bait of cane-pole fishermen and countless fly-rodders who have embarrassed many a dry-fly purist.

What are splake?

Splake are trout hybrids, a cross between lake and brook trout. Splake are raised expressly by hatcheries to replenish understocked lakes, since they grow rapidly, have a long life, and possess ideal game characteristics. They strike viciously, possess great stamina, and execute spectacular leaps. Splake are excellent eating and reach 8 pounds after 7 years.

LAKE TROUT

How large do lake trout get?

One-hundred-pounders are occasionally reported by commercial fishermen.

What do the keepers of the official rod-and-reel records say?

A world's-record lake trout, caught in Great Bear Lake, Northwest Territories, Canada, in 1970, weighed 65 pounds.

When is the best time of year to fish for lake trout?

When the ice begins to move out, start casting along the shoreline. Trout are hungry now and will hit anything from flies to plugs and spinners. When they leave the deep water in the fall and return to the shallows to spawn, you can hit them again with the same lures. But all in all, spring is the best time, since they have voracious appetites after the long winter freeze.

Can you fish for lake trout through the ice?

Sure, if you know their haunts and don't mind the inconvenience. Don't forget, the farther north you go, the colder the temperature and the thicker the ice! You must be familiar with the aquatic terrain, so that you don't wind up doing more ice chopping than fishing—especially in the shallows where the water freezes all the way to the bottom!

What are some of the names given to lake trout?

Since lake trout are distributed over a great area of North America, countless names have been given to this species by Americans, Canadians, and Indians. Therefore, we have such regional names as mackinaw trout, salmon trout, forktail trout, togue, namaycush, gray trout, and a host of others.

What is the range of lake trout?

From New England across the northern states to California and north to the Arctic Circle.

Are there any subspecies of lake trout?

Yes, the siscowet, an inhabitant of the Great Lakes. It lives in extremely deep water at depths of 300 to 600 feet and is seldom caught by any method other than commercial.

How cold must the water be for lake trout to thrive?

A little above freezing! Lake trout prefer water temperatures of 40 to 50 degrees F. and are rarely found in lakes less than 40 feet deep.

Then why are lake trout found in 10-foot depths along the shoreline of streams?

True, they *are* found in these shallows, but only during the spring after the ice breaks up or in the fall when the shallows begin to chill. Trout move about freely and sometimes leave a lake or tributary stream to feed. Naturally, during warm weather, lake trout inhabit only the deeper levels of the lake. But in the northernmost lakes, the water remains cold enough for you to find them in the shallows much of the time.

What are the spawning habits of lake trout?

Unlike most other trout, lake trout spawn in the fall, from September to December. Spawning takes place in deep water (100 feet or more in the larger lakes) and in the shallows of smaller lakes. The ritual of spawning is almost a community affair. Small groups of males will fertilize the eggs of one or more females. The eggs are deposited over rocky or gravel bottoms. The incubation period is about 44 days at 50 degrees F. and 160 days at 37 degrees F. The eggs are left unguarded, and after hatching, the young are on their own.

THE QUARRY

Recently I noticed an obvious absence of lake trout in many of the cold, deep-water lakes in Canada and Alaska. From all indications, the environment seemed to be ideally suited to support a good population, and yet no signs of trout activity were present. What is the reason for this?

One main reason for a lake's inability to support trout is an inadequate supply of oxygen at the bottom levels. Some lakes contain a profusion of decaying vegetation such as tree trunks and leaves. If the rate of decomposition is great, then the consumption of oxygen could be enough to make the bottom uninhabitable. Lake trout, whose survival depends upon cold water, must descend to deep water in the many lakes whose surface levels are warmed by the summer sun.

What do lake trout eat?

Lake trout are hardy feeders and eat practically any natural aquatic food that thrives in their habitat.

Shallow-water lake trout feed upon flies, other insects, and crustaceans. Deep-water trout feed primarily upon small fishes such as herring, smelts, whitefish, eels, and sculpins.

What angling methods can be used to catch lake trout?

There are different ways to catch lake trout at a given time, in a specific place. For example, lake trout that inhabit the far north waters where the water temperatures are cold enough to keep them near the surface or in the shallows during the summer months can be caught using spin, plug, and even fly-casting gear. Surface trolling too will take lake trout, but the heavy, cumbersome lines and weights are unnecessary.

If you are fishing for them in the southern part of their range during the hot summer months, you've got to troll deep to score, because that's where they are—100 feet or more down.

Now, then, during the spring or fall the waters are cooler, so the farther north you are, the cooler the water and the more likely that Mr. Trout will be foraging in the shallows. Here is

During the summer, lake trout
inhabit deep water, so you must
troll slowly, using weighted lines
or heavy deep-running lures to
reach them. The distended belly of
this one was filled with snails, but
it couldn't resist a weighted
Hopkins lure in Muncho Lake,
British Columbia. (HAL SCHARP)

where you can hit him with your streamers, spinners, and
plugs. He'll eat them up, and you'll have a great time using
light tackle. Just be sure to wear warm clothes!

**What kind of trolling gear should I use to catch big lake trout
during the summer at the southern limits of their range?**

This means they're really deep, so you've got to be prepared
to use a heavy, practical outfit and forgo any notions about
taking trout in a sporting manner. Lines such as braided steel,
copper, lead-core, and Monel will all get you down deep. Sin-
gle-strand soft-drawn Monel seems to be the most popular,
since it is least likely to kink, is heavy enough to be efficient,
and comes in many line tests. Don't choose the line test to
match the size of the fish you expect to catch; just get line
heavy enough to reach the desired depth.

Natural baits such as herring, whitefish, chubs, and smelts
are often used for trolling. The baits should be rigged so that

they spin or rotate rather than glide through the water as a fish does normally. Believe it or not, trout like it this way and, if hungry, antagonized, or whatever, will pounce upon it with gusto. Some anglers rig additional attractors in the form of spinners (the double Indiana spinner is very effective) in front of the baitfish. Spoons too are popular and, possibly, more widely used. Big spoons trolled slowly over trout territory seldom miss a hookup.

Supposing I want to catch big lake trout—you know the kind: those fantastic lunkers pictured in Canadian Government brochures. Are there really any left? If so, how do I connect?

I'll admit they're becoming more scarce every day, because many of the provinces sanction commercial fishing. There are still a few husky ones around, but you'll have to fly into extreme-northern wilderness lakes to find 'em. Even so, you'll have to work harder to catch one than you did 30 years ago!

Nowadays, if you want big trout, you need a floatplane and an Eskimo guide. These lunkers were caught above the Arctic Circle in the Northwest Territories. (CANADIAN TRAVEL BUREAU)

DOLLY VARDEN TROUT

What are the likely haunts of the Dolly Varden?

Dolly Vardens are found west of the Rocky Mountains from northern California to Alaska. Freshwater Dollys are plentiful in the lakes of British Columbia. In salt water, Dollys are found in British Columbia and Alaska.

How did the Dolly Varden trout get its name?

The Dolly Varden trout received its name from a female character in Charles Dickens' novel *Barnaby Rudge*. Miss Varden wore a pink-spotted dress.

What are some other names for Dolly Vardens?

Bull trout and Dollys.

What distinguishes the Dolly Varden from the true trout species?

Its teeth are located only in the anterior part of the roof of the mouth, with none in the rear. This identifies it as a true char.

What is the rod-and-reel world's record for Dolly Varden trout?

A 32-pounder was caught in Lake Pend Oreille, Idaho, in 1949.

What are some of the Dolly Varden's habits?

Dolly Vardens are gluttonous feeders, wolfing down almost anything that will fit into their mouths. At one time they were vilified for feeding upon the eggs of trout and salmon. Even the Alaska conservation department gave a bounty for their capture until it discovered that the Dollys were actually contributing to the propagation of salmon and not destroying them. Dollys eat the free-floating, unfertilized eggs of the salmon rather than the fertilized eggs which lie hidden in the crevices of the gravel bottom. Dollys were also found consuming large numbers of bullheads and sticklebacks, the real criminals which gorge themselves upon the fertilized eggs of the trout and salmon.

Still, some anglers scorn the Dollys for their cannibalistic tendency to eat salmon fingerlings.

Where are Dolly Vardens found?

Dollys are found in lakes where sandbars drop off into deep water and on the bottom edges of underwater reefs. In the streams, they like eddies, riffles, and deep pools, where they are found lying on the bottom. They are also encountered around any kind of obstruction in the current, such as logs, fallen trees, and boulders.

What are the spawning habits of the Dolly Varden?

Like other members of the salmon family, Dollys spawn in the fall in gravel-bottomed streams. The female prepares the nest (redd) and, after spawning, covers the eggs with gravel. Sea-running Dollys usually return to the sea or inhabit deep pools in the stream in which they spawn.

How does the Dolly Varden rank as game?

It is a fine sport fish and is comparable, pound for pound, to many other chars and trouts. It is eager in its assault upon any artificial lures and puts up a pretty good scrap, especially on light tackle.

ARCTIC CHAR

What is the range and distribution of the Arctic char?

The distribution of the Arctic char is circumpolar. Both anadromous and landlocked variety are found only in the northern reaches of the Western and Eastern Hemispheres. As their name implies, these wilderness fish inhabit only the cold waters bordering on or north of the Arctic Circle.

How much did the world's rod-and-reel-record Arctic char weigh?

A 29-pound-11-ounce specimen was taken at Great Bear Lake, Northwest Territories, Canada.

Is there any consistency in the sizes of the landlocked and sea-run Arctic chars?

The sea-run variety outweighs the landlocked by many pounds. The landlocked usually weighs only 3 to 6 pounds, while the sea-run models average 10 to 12 pounds, with 15-pounders common.

What do Arctic chars feed on?

Crustaceans, sculpins, sand eels, and capelin make up the major part of their diet, while insects become a supplement as the Arctic chars move inland.

THE QUARRY After their general location has been established, where are the best places to look for Arctic chars?

Arctic chars like fast water. They will be found in the shallow riffles next to gravel or sand bars. The mouths of rivers and estuaries are also good spots.

Are they difficult to catch?

Arctic chars possess voracious appetites and gulp practically all artificial lures with enthusiasm. Since cautionary instincts seem to be absent in this species, they're a real fun fish to catch and you don't need much know-how. Fly, spinning, and plug casting will catch all the Arctic char you want—once you find them.

What kind of planning is necessary for an Arctic char fishing trip?

You'll have to decide whether you want to fish for the landlocked or the anadromous kind. The landlocked variety are much smaller fish, but you have a wider latitude when choosing your time and location. If you're after the sea-run biggies, then it is important for you to know their movements, since this variety does not linger long in one place and your action could be limited to only one or two weeks. Base your advance arrangements upon the fish's probable arrival.

7

The Salmons

ATLANTIC SALMON

Please describe the fighting qualities of the Atlantic salmon and explain why this fish is one of the most sought after among fly fishermen.

The Atlantic salmon is no ordinary fish! To preserve this great warrior, many communities have passed special legislation with strict rules regarding the manner in which it can be caught. For instance, in some areas anglers may not use average sporting tackle. Only fly-fishing tackle and techniques are allowed. Even flies with weights are prohibited. These rigid laws are in effect almost everywhere throughout the North American continent. This increases the difficulty of catching the fish and presents a greater challenge to the angler.

The Atlantic salmon is prized because it has all the qualities that great fighting fish possess: strength, leaping ability, endurance, and spirit!

What is the present world's record for Atlantic salmon taken on rod and reel?

A 79-pound-2-ounce beauty was caught in the Tana River, Norway, in 1928.

What expenses can I expect to incur if I want to fish for Atlantic salmon in some of the Canadian provinces?

Pursuing Atlantic salmon can be mighty expensive. It is an exclusive sport that only a small number of anglers can afford. Lodging, guides' fees, boat rentals, etc. all add up, so that most of the expense is incurred during the time you are waiting for the salmon. Experts recommend that an angler allow a full month to wait for acceptable water and weather conditions. After that, only a week or ten days of good or excellent fishing action can be expected. You fish selected areas—either pools or "beats." Early salmon fishing is April/May for black salmon; late June through September for bright, or silver, salmon. You reserve a week's fishing in advance with the owners of the runs or pools.

All this adds up to one bit of advice: salmon fishing is the most unpredictable sport going for anglers, so don't expect any guarantees. How much does all this cost? It could easily amount to $1,000 for two weeks. If you're lucky, really lucky, you might hit the action at the prime time, get your fill in a few days, and come out under a couple of hundred dollars. But don't count on it!

Is it true that in some Canadian provinces a hired guide must accompany a nonresident angler on any salmon trip?

Yes. In the provinces of Quebec and New Brunswick, guides are required by law for a nonresident angler, whether he is fishing in a boat or from the shoreline.

In Newfoundland, nonresident anglers must be accompanied by a guide except when fishing one-quarter mile upstream or one-quarter mile downstream from the Trans-Canada Highway bridges crossing scheduled streams.

Nova Scotia has excellent sport fishing for salmon, but here again a registered guide must accompany a nonresident angler.

In comparison, Prince Edward Island has a modest salmon sport fishery, but guides are not required by law.

What are some of the differences between the Atlantic salmon and the Pacific salmon?

One of the chief differences is in their breeding and migratory habits. Both species spend their lives in the ocean and return to fresh water (sometimes over 1,000 miles) to spawn. The Pacific salmon, however (five distinct species), all die shortly after spawning. The Atlantic salmon (one species) returns to the ocean and lives to spawn again.

The Pacific salmon, particularly the Chinook, is much larger than the Atlantic species. It may spend 4 to 6 years in the sea before it begins its final migration to the spawning grounds.

How long does a young Atlantic salmon remain in fresh water before migrating to the open ocean?

Juvenile salmon could remain in the freshwater streams anywhere from 1 to 4 years before beginning their journey to the sea, where they will grow much larger. Depending upon geography and heredity, young salmon (parr) could be only 5 or 6 inches long when they enter the ocean. Young salmon over 6 inches in length are called smolts. Some will begin their journey after 2 or 3 years, with the largest 2-year-olds migrating first. Still others will remain in fresh water for 4 years before heading for the ocean. There is no perceptible uniform pattern to their movements, age, and growth rate.

It has been proved that salmon are able to return to the exact location of their birth in freshwater streams. How do they accomplish this?

Scientists agree that since fresh water contains countless chemical and physical substances, salmon coming from the sea are oriented by using their acute olfactory sense. As they travel to their ancestral breeding grounds, they are able to detect the difference between one water area and another.

Well, then, how do you account for salmon's orientation in the sea a thousand miles away from the freshwater entrance to their birthplace?

So far, scientists cannot explain the extraordinary navigational abilities of the salmon while at sea. There are theories involving various homing mechanisms, such as the fish's ability to detect gravitational variations which help them find their way to their spawning grounds. However, despite extensive research in the field, scientists have been unable to arrive at a simple explanation for this remarkable phenomenon.

What is the growth rate of the Atlantic salmon?

It is strange how slowly Atlantic salmon grow during the first years of development and feeding in the streams. After several years they are only 5 to 7 inches long (smolts) just before they enter the sea. After a year in the ocean (and, no doubt, a tremendous amount of feeding) they measure about 24 inches. After 2 years, 30 inches, and at the end of 3 full years, 40 inches and 30 pounds or more!

If Atlantic salmon don't feed in fresh water, how is it possible to get them to take a bait?

While en route to their spawning grounds, salmon do not feed, since they have fed well in the ocean and conditioned

themselves for the long fast. If and when they strike a bait or
lure, it is just a reflex and not a desire to feed. Here is where
the trick comes in—to tantalize them enough so that they
strike in anger.

**Have any salmon been tagged to determine the length and
time of their migrations to and from the sea?**

The longest Atlantic salmon migration on record was made
by a 5-year-old river smolt that was tagged in May 1959 in a
New Brunswick river and recovered in October 1960 off the
coast of Greenland.

**In negotiating the freshwater tributaries to its breeding
grounds, what kind of resting places does the Atlantic salmon
choose?**

Salmon are found resting in certain pools of big rivers,

Because of the irregular, rocky terrain and swift waters of the Rivière
Madeleine in Quebec, salmon anglers are permitted to use spinning
tackle instead of the fly-fishing gear that is rigidly enforced elsewhere. Spinners and spoons are most effective lures when worked in
turbulent white water. (HAL SCHARP)

streams, and small brooks. They seem to choose the same pools used by their predecessors when similar water conditions existed. Salmon will move about from lie to lie (resting stations) as the water levels change. During their journey upstream, they may be casual in their efforts to reach their birthplace or they may be in a hurry. It is difficult to understand the erratic movements of salmon and their choices of aquatic communities.

If I'm in an area where salmon may be taken only by fly-fishing methods, what kind of tackle should I use?

If you're accustomed to a fly rod, you might be best off using your own tackle—gear that you've been fishing with for years, so that you know its limits. One thing, though: you'll have to use an extra-large reel, one that can accommodate at least 200 yards of 15- or 20-pound-test braided Dacron line backing. Fishing for salmon in open stretches, plus their ability to execute tremendously long and swift runs, will require plenty of line, a smooth drag mechanism, and, of course, the main prerequisites—experience and skill.

If you're not familiar with fly fishing, choose a 7-ounce rod with a detachable butt (for leverage and also for easier reeling when you're playing your fish). A 9-foot rod is preferred by most salmon fishermen. Large flies must be cast a long distance and picked up with minimum effort, so a tapered line WF-8-F or WF-9-F is recommended.

Now you must learn to use it. Practice well before making that expedition you're dreaming about.

How do you land salmon?

There are several ways. The experts are able to land salmon by grabbing the caudal peduncle (the narrow part of the tail) by hand and hoisting them out of the water. This is not for beginners!

Most anglers use either a net or a tailer, but some nets are bulky and awkward to use when large salmon are running. A tailer is a simple snare which, when placed around the fish's tail, serves as a lasso. Then the angler can hoist his prize from the water into the boat or drag it ashore.

Although gaff hooks are permitted in some places, their use is frowned upon. In other areas, they are prohibited.

What kinds of flies are popular among salmon anglers?

Wet-fly patterns such as Dusty Miller, Green Highlander, Jock Scott, Durham Ranger, Black Dose, Silver Grey, Silver Rat, Silver Wilkinson, Red Abbey, and Lady Amhurst are some of the favorites in a variety of sizes from No. 8 to No. 6/0 hooks.

Some acceptable dry flies are the Royal Wulff, White Wulff, Irresistible, Rat Faced McDougal, Surface Stonefly, and Pink Lady, in various hook sizes.

When, and under what conditions, are salmon easiest to catch?

The longer salmon stay in the river or stream after returning from the sea, the more cautious and wary they become. They're less cautious and will take a fly more eagerly when they first come in from the sea.

PACIFIC SALMON

How do the fighting qualities of the Pacific salmon compare with those of the Atlantic salmon?

None of the Pacific salmon except the Chinook and the silver (coho) exhibit any real fighting characteristics worthy of comparison. These two species, if fished for in the streams with fly tackle only, might present an interesting challenge to the angler. Under these conditions, the Chinook and silver salmon could come close to matching the sporting qualities of the highly elusive Atlantic salmon.

Are sport-fishing regulations as strict for the Pacific salmon as they are for the Atlantic?

No. Except for occasional scheduled stream and saltwater time limits, anglers enjoy almost complete freedom in fishing for the various species of Pacific salmon.

However, temporary and periodic restrictions are placed upon certain small areas where authorities believe the fishing pressure may be great enough to cause a drop in future populations.

How large do Chinook salmon get, and what is the world's rod-and-reel record?

The Skeena River, British Columbia, Canada, produced one in 1959 that weighed 92 pounds. Many Chinook salmon weighing over 125 pounds have been caught by commercial methods.

What other names are given to the Chinook salmon?

Regional names such as king, spring, and tyee salmon are often used. Tyee is a Siwash Indian word meaning "chief," and it refers, in this case, to size. The world-famous Tyee Club at Campbell River, British Columbia, Canada, defines a tyee as any Chinook salmon over 30 pounds.

How many kinds of Pacific salmon are there?

There are five species found from northeastern Alaska to San Francisco: Chinook (also called king), sockeye (red), coho (silver), pink (humpback), and chum (dog).

Chinooks, the largest of the group, average 20 to 25 pounds and sometimes reach 100 pounds or more. Pink salmon are the smallest—averaging about 3 pounds.

The coho and Chinook are the most popular with anglers. In salt water they are usually caught by trolling methods. In freshwater lakes, trolling, spinning, or spin- and bait-casting are used. Rivers and streams lure the fly caster, for in this environment the salmon really exhibits its gamy characteristics and creates a challenge for the angler.

What is the natural life cycle of the Pacific salmon?

Pacific salmon are anadromous—that is, they spend most of their lives in the ocean, but after two to four years of maturity they ascend freshwater rivers to spawn. After traveling hundreds, and sometimes thousands, of miles, salmon return to their ancestral spawning grounds. When they reach their grounds, eggs are deposited in "redds," or gravel nests. Each female produces up to 8,000 eggs, depending upon species and size. After the fall spawning is completed, both male and female die. When the eggs hatch in the spring, the young salmon may begin their downstream migration at once or remain in the streams a year or more. Some sockeye salmon stay in lakes during their entire lives.

Since predators, floods, silt, temperature variances, and drought destroy many eggs and young fingerlings, the salmon that reach the sea are probably less than 10 percent of the number of eggs spawned.

What is the range of the Chinook salmon in North America?

Along the Pacific coast, the Chinook is found from Monterey Bay, California, to Alaska. It also ranges on the other side of the Pacific from the Bering Strait south through Russia and Japan to northern China. Chinooks have been introduced successfully in New Zealand and Chile.

What is the main diet of the Chinook salmon before they migrate to the sea, and what do they feed upon during their time in the sea?

Before they migrate, they feed on freshwater aquatic creatures such as crustaceans, worms, flies, and other insects.

In the ocean, Chinooks prey upon small fishes such as herring, anchovies, and sardines—supplemented with squids, shrimp, and other crustaceans.

Is it true that salmon stop feeding when they enter fresh water to begin their journey to the spawning grounds?

During their lives spent in the ocean, they eat enough to prepare for the arduous upstream journey. Stored fats provide sustenance for developing eggs and milt and the energy to negotiate the many miles of a perilous trip.

How far does the Chinook salmon travel in its migration?

Records indicate that some Chinooks travel as far as 2,000 miles from the sea into the Yukon and its tributaries.

How can I tell the difference between young Chinook salmon in fresh water and the other species?

Young Chinooks (called parr) have vertical bars and, occasionally, oval markings almost bisected by the lateral line. The parr marks are usually wider than the interspaces. These markings separate them from the silver (coho), red, pink, and chum (dog) salmon.

What happens to the young Chinook fry after they hatch in the streams?

Young Chinook fry may go to the sea soon after hatching, or they may remain in a lake or river for a year or two before making their journey to the sea. They may be taken accidentally by anglers using flies or spinners and offer fair sport.

Slow-trolling of a large, beaded teaspoon spinner can hook giant Chinook salmon like this 69-pounder taken by the author in Cook Inlet, Alaska. When salmon of this species leave the sea, prior to their journey upstream to spawn, dramatic changes in physiology and color take place. The male's jaw becomes grotesquely hooked and his color changes to dark red. (MARY SCHARP)

How do anglers catch most of their Chinook and silver salmon? And where?

Trolling or drifting in the ocean near shore, in protected sounds, bays, and straits or in river estuaries.

What kind of tackle and baits do they use?

Saltwater trolling is done with spoons, large plugs, and natural baits such as herring, anchovies, candlefish, and Pacific sardines.

All trolling should be slow, so that the spoons and plugs barely wobble. The natural baitfish must be rigged on double hooks in tandem in such a manner that it gyrates slowly through the water. In order to catch the salmon's attention, the bait must appear to be disabled. Special accessories (such as a large shiny metal flasher called a Herring Dodger), placed between a sinker and the bait to tease a salmon into striking, have been very successful.

Drifting with the above baits and lures is also effective, provided both the current and the wind are cooperative enough to keep the bait moving properly through the water.

Rods are a matter of choice. A medium conventional trolley rod or a boat rod with a star-drag reel and 30- to 40-pound-test line is standard equipment. A medium saltwater spinning rod 6½ to 7½ feet in length may be used with a large saltwater spinning reel holding at least 300 yards of 20-pound-test line. Larger rods can be awkward in landing your fish.

What's the best way to land a Chinook salmon if I'm fishing from a boat?

West Coast anglers favor a large landing net or a gaff hook.

What signs do I look for to locate Chinook salmon in salt water?

Anglers usually remember where salmon have been found in former years. Local inquiries will probably give you valuable information as to the salmons' whereabouts. These areas can then be observed for feeding fish coming to the surface. Gulls too may announce the arrival of salmon. Tide rips and mouths of rivers are often productive spots.

Do tidal changes and the time of day influence the salmon's location and feeding habits?

Yes. The angler whose lines are in the water at daybreak will reap the benefit. Incoming tides along the coastal waters and river mouths seem to spark a salmon's desire to feed.

What fishing methods are used for catching Chinooks in the freshwater streams?

Drifting with gobs of salmon eggs into holes where salmon

This Michigan Chinook salmon fell for a fly-rod-sized spoon. Migration to parent streams begins in late summer, with heavy concentration at stream mouths. The action peaks sometime in September—at the onset of spawning runs.

may be lying is one of the more popular methods. These rigs are standard lures which come with spinners in a variety of styles. Although it is presumed that salmon don't feed after they begin their journey upstream, the lures are designed to attract their attention or to annoy them into striking out of anger or habit.

"Tee" spoons in various sizes and finishes, spinners, and spoons trolled or drifted are all productive.

What methods are used to catch coho (silver) salmon in salt water and in freshwater streams?

The same methods and techniques that apply to catching Chinook salmon. However, the weight of rods, line tests, and lure sizes might be a little on the heavy side for cohos, since they are a much smaller fish. Using lighter tackle will enhance the sporting value of catching these fine fish.

What do coho salmon average in weight, and what is the world's rod-and-reel record?

Coho salmon average about 8 to 9 pounds. A record 31-pounder was caught in Cowichan Bay, British Columbia, Canada, in 1947.

8

The Grab Bag

CATFISH

How many major species of catfish are there, and what are their record rod-and-reel weights?

There are three major species. A blue catfish weighed in at a whoppin' 97 pounds and was caught in the Missami River, South Dakota, in 1959.

In 1964, a channel catfish weighing 58 pounds was taken from the Santee-Cooper Reservoir, South Carolina.

A flathead catfish weighing 79 pounds 8 ounces was caught in White River, Indiana, in 1966.

How big do the largest of these catfish species get?

Blue catfish are the largest and can weigh up to 160 pounds.

Which of the three species of catfish is thought to possess the strongest fighting qualities, and why?

The blue catfish is by far the "tiger" of the clan. It doesn't tolerate turbid, algae-choked bodies of water and prefers clear, swift streams and clean sandy or gravel lake bottoms. Its choice of water conditions may be the reason for its superior fighting abilities and for the absence of the sluggishness that is characteristic of the other species.

What is the range of the blue catfish?

The blue catfish ranges from southern Canada and the Great Lakes region to the Gulf states and from the Appalachian Mountains west through the Mississippi Valley, including its many tributary streams. It is also found in the large streams of Mexico.

What is the natural food of the blue catfish?

There is little that this critter will refuse, but he prefers fish, crayfish, mussels, clams, insects, and worms.

When do catfish spawn?

Late in April and through May. They have the unique ability to lay their eggs whenever they wish during this period. They usually pick a time that offers suitable water conditions, such as low and clean water.

What is the function of the thin, whiskerlike appendages on the nose and lower jaw of a catfish?

These appendages (barbels) are actually taste buds or receptors. Since all catfish are bottom feeders, nature provided them with equipment that makes it easier for them to feed in murky or muddy water.

CARP

How big do carp get, and what is the world's record on rod and reel?

Carp weighing 60 to 70 pounds are often netted by state fishery-management personnel during their lake-cleaning operations to remove "rough" fish.

A 55-pound-5-ounce carp was caught at Clearwater Lake, Minnesota, in 1952 with rod and reel.

What is the range of carp?

Carp are widely distributed from southern Canada south to the Gulf states and coast to coast in the United States. They are also found in Mexico and Central and South America.

Under what conditions do carp thrive best?

Carp are hardy creatures and can thrive under conditions that other fish find impossible. Carp even survive pollution and stagnation that kill most other fish species. They have a tolerance for all kinds of muddy bottoms containing an abundance of vegetation and organic matter found in slow-moving rivers, lakes, and ponds.

What are carp's feeding habits?

Carp are omnivorous feeders which forage on insect larvae, plankton, worms, crustaceans, and vegetation.

When were carp introduced into this country, and by whom?

Carp were first successfully introduced into the United States in 1876 by the United States Fish Commission. Although they came from Germany, they were really indigenous to Asia and became widespread in Europe centuries before Christ.

To what family of fishes does the carp belong?

Carp are the largest of the minnow family in North and South America.

Are they a game fish?

Not in a sporting sense. They rarely take an artificial bait. They are a slovenly, sluggish type of creature who, because of sheer weight alone, offer some resistance to capture. Carp can be fun, though. With the use of light tackle, the quest can take on the character of a mild sporting event.

What kind of bait and terminal rig is popular among carp anglers?

Dough molded into a ball and compressed on a treble hook (hiding the hooks) is the most popular bait. Soaked stale corn kernels are also excellent bait for carp and should be strung on a single hook (No. 4 or No. 5) like beads on a necklace.

For casting and bottom-fishing purposes, a sliding egg sinker should be used. To prevent the sinker from sliding down to the bait, simply tie a knot or two about 12 inches above it. Carp usually take their time and mouth the bait first a few times, so they shouldn't be struck at the first pickup. The egg sinker allows the line and bait to slide along without any restriction as the carp nibbles the bait. If he feels any restraint he will drop it immediately, so give him slack and time before setting the hook.

How do you make the dough bait for carp fishing?

The dough bait (usually called "dough balls") is made from equal parts of cornmeal and white flour, mixed with small amounts of sugar, honey, or molasses and enough water to hold it together. The dough should be heated over a slow fire for about five minutes and be worked with the hands while warming. The mixture should be kneaded like bread dough for 10 or 15 minutes until it is shaped into a good-sized, firm ball. For different bait sizes just pull off a chunk and mold it onto the hook.

Are carp detrimental to a community that also contains game fishes such as bass, sunfish, and pike?

Carp are not popular among most anglers because of their bad habit of wallowing around in the shallows, uprooting vegetation and muddying the water. Although carp don't prey upon fish or their spawn, they are indirectly responsible for disturbing, and often destroying, the delicate spawn of game fish.

What are the spawning habits of carp?

Carp are prolific in their spawning, which accounts for their consistent and successful propagation throughout North America.

Carp spawn in shallow water during the late spring. The female is capable of broadcasting as many as 2,000,000 eggs. Under normal conditions, a young carp will reach 8 or 9 inches in the first year.

Are carp good to eat?

Yes, but they are bony. Special culinary techniques will evidently make carp tasty, since 19,000,000 pounds were marketed in the United States during one year.

STURGEON

How many species make up the family of sturgeons?

Sixteen species of sturgeon are distributed throughout the world. Seven species occur in North America.

Which species of sturgeon is the most popular with anglers in North America?

The white sturgeon, largest of North America's freshwater fishes, is the most sought after by anglers.

How big do sturgeons get, and what is the rod-and-reel world's record?

There are some real giants around. One that was caught commercially was reported to weigh 1,800 pounds! The rod-and-reel record stands at a mere 360 pounds. The fish was caught in the Snake River, Idaho, in 1956.

What is the range and distribution of white sturgeons?

They range along the Pacific coast from Monterey, California, north to Alaska. They spend a good part of their lives in the ocean and enter the larger tributaries to spawn. Some are landlocked in areas such as the upper Columbia River headwaters.

What are the white sturgeon's spawning habits?

White sturgeons take about 12 to 20 years to mature. During this time they live in the ocean or in brackish water until, as adults, they begin their yearly migration into the rivers to spawn. Breeding takes place in the spring over gravel beds.

During the summer months, they swim downstream and return to the ocean. The female is capable of depositing hundreds of thousands of eggs, which are ignored and left at the mercy of predators. The roe of sturgeons (caviar) is especially valuable, and the flesh is highly palatable.

How old do white sturgeons become, and what is their rate of growth?

White sturgeons that reach 15 feet are estimated at 65 to 75 years old.

In the second year, they will reach 19 inches. By the seventh year, 40 inches. By the time they are 12 years old, they may have reached maturity and will measure about 52 inches. After maturity, the average growth is about 2½ inches per year.

What do sturgeons feed on?

Sturgeons are slow-moving, scavengerlike fish who feed upon snails, mollusks, and an occasional smelt.

Lamprey eels, suckers, and sardines are popular fresh baits used to catch giant-size sturgeons— generally considered the largest of the freshwater fishes. Monsters like this, exceeding 100 pounds, are found deep in the rivers and lakes of North America. (FLORIDA GAME & FRESH WATER COMMISSION)

How are sturgeons caught with rod and reel?

Heavy equipment should be used, since the species reaches great proportions. Although the general population of white sturgeons is diminishing rapidly, it is common to catch large, mature specimens that weigh 75 to 100 pounds.

Cut bait made from suckers or other river-bottom fishes is good. Sturgeons will take lamprey eels or night crawlers eagerly.

SHAD

How big do American shad get, and what kind of challenge do they offer to the angler?

The American shad, also know as white shad, Atlantic shad, jack, silver herring, and hickory shad, range up to 8 pounds. Twelve-pounders have been reported, but these catches are exceptional.

As with almost any fish, the shad's game qualities can best be measured by the manner in which it is caught. Light tackle provides more interesting action and, coupled with the use of artificial lures, presents a greater challenge to the angler. Fly fishing for shad is a terrific sport, and under ideal conditions it is comparable to trout fishing with flies.

Where are shad found, and what is their range?

Shad are anadromous fish like salmon. That is, they spend most of their lives in the sea. They are usually caught as they ascend coastal rivers and streams to spawn.

They are found on both coasts of the United States. On the Pacific, they range from southern Alaska to southern California, with heavy populations in the San Francisco Bay area. On the Atlantic coast, shad range from northern Florida to the

Gulf of St. Lawrence. The heaviest action is usually in Connecticut rivers (Salmon, Connecticut, Scantic, Eight Mile, and East) during the month of May when the run reaches its peak. In the South, the St. John's River in Florida is a top producer of shad. Although they begin entering the Florida tributaries in early December, the peak of the run is in March.

American shad prefer to spawn in the main rivers along the coasts, while the hickory shad seek smaller tributary streams.

What kind of tackle and bait are recommended for catching shad?

Shad (sometimes called the "poor man's salmon") are fairly flexible fish that will take a variety of artificial lures such as spoons, jigs, spinners, and flies. They will also hit natural baits like grass shrimp, minnows, and worms, but anglers seem to have better luck using the flashy lures.

Try trolling with a light bait-casting or spinning rod or casting (if conditions permit) with reflective spoons or spinners. The No. 00 Drone type of spoon, worked close to the bottom, is most effective if you impart erratic action to the lure.

White or yellow bucktail jigs and the silver wobbling-type spoons are the most popular among the spinning or bait-casting aficionados. Shad prefer little lures, so stay with the smaller spoons and don't use jigs over ¼ ounce.

The use of fly-fishing tackle is ideal for catching shad. In shallow streams the angler should use a sinking line and wet flies; but if the water is running deep, the flies must be weighted in order to reach the shad on the bottom. Under these circumstances, beaded flies are more effective.

Since a shad's mouth is delicately constructed, hooks pull out easily. Therefore, special care must be taken when you're setting the hook. Large nets are a must for landing shad.

PART TWO

Tackle,
Bait, and
Technique

What kind of fishing tackle did primitive man use to catch his fish, and how did it work?

Ancient man used a handline made of a lightweight vine, tied to a "gorge"—the forerunner of today's hook. Archaeologists discovered the first fishing-hook gorges under 22 feet of earth in a peat bed in France.

Some gorges, estimated at over 7,000 years old, were made of slender bones, shells, pieces of wood, and stones. They were simple crossbars tapered to a sharp point at each end, with a notch in the middle where the "line" was fastened. A bait was fixed to the gorge so that the line lay parallel to it, making it easy for a fish to swallow the offering. A sharp tug on the line would free the gorge from the bait and cause it to lodge crosswise in the fish's gullet. Then the angler could drag in his quarry.

When did man begin to use artificial lures, and what were they made of?

Roman records from about A.D. 200 give accounts of the Macedonians' fishing with artificial flies made from red wool and the feathers that grow under a cock's wattles.

Did they fish for sport in those early days?

Presumably so. The use of a lure by an angler has always been thought of as an exercise in patience and a challenge directed to one fish. Food fishermen, like Simon Peter of Galilee, usually caught fish in quantity by using nets, traps, or other devices that were more productive and profitable.

Early Egyptian pictures show people fishing in what appears to be a man-made fish tank. Were they fishing for sport or for food?

Essentially for sport, since fish were plentiful in those days. Like the wealthy Romans who built special fish ponds, the Egyptian royalty also enjoyed the convenience of guaranteed fish action. This may have been the beginning of fish culture in both societies and a forerunner of our present stocking practices in streams and ponds. Today's affluent angler might be considered a counterpart of the ancient upper-income anglers of Rome and Egypt.

Is Izaak Walton's book *The Compleat Angler* the earliest authentic literature on fishing for sport?

No. Dame Juliana Berners' essay "The Treatyse of Fishing with an Angle" (*Boke of St. Albans*) was written in 1496 and is considered the first contribution to angling literature. This work was followed by *The Arte of Angling,* published in 1577, which was lost for centuries until its recent discovery. Sir

Izaak's famous book (with a second part by Charles Cotton) was not published until 1676.

I'm told that the anglerfish was using a lure to catch fish before man ever thought of it. How does he do this?

The anglerfish (*Lophias piscatorius*) is the most common of several species of seagoing Izaak Waltons. It is a bottom dweller and is widespread in the Atlantic and Pacific Oceans in the temperate zones only.

This fellow has the unique ability to attract small fish by wiggling his lures from a fish pole, bringing the unsuspecting victim close enough so that it can be engulfed.

An anglerfish may reach 4 feet and weigh up to 70 pounds. He is well camouflaged to blend with his environment. His fishing pole is formed of the first dorsal spine, which is located on the snout and overhangs the mouth. He can move it, and the lure, which consists of small, wormlike tentacles, will wiggle to attract fish. He allows the fish to nibble on the lure while, at the same time, he moves the pole so that his quarry is in a position to be gulped.

If fly fishing is so popular and offers such a great challenge to anglers taking game fish, why aren't more anglers practicing it?

Compared with other methods of angling, fly fishing is the most difficult to learn and requires the greatest skill. As one of the oldest and most complex methods of catching fish, it involves strenuous work and demands a lot of patience and determination. Failures can cause quick exasperation.

Fly fishing is the most artistic way to fish, requiring finesse and a good working knowledge of a fish's food supply. When a fly fisherman catches a fish, he knows that he has applied his expertise and has given his quarry a fair chance.

Unfortunately, most anglers won't pay the price of catching fish the hard way when they can use easier methods that increase their productivity. In a capsule, they are not conditioned psychologically to catching fish by a method that requires creativeness, cogitation, and study.

How many types of fly lines are there, and what are their uses?

There are three—known as level, weight-forward, and double-taper—each serving a particular purpose. The level line is the least expensive but a little more difficult to handle than the others. Its diameter is constant from one end to the other.

A weight-forward line is the most expensive, but it is easier to cast—especially when you're striving for distance. The line is made with a thin section for a few feet, then a thick, heavy "shooting line." Obviously, the heavier line is easier to cast once the thick portion of line (shooting head) has cleared the rod guides. Sometimes this type of line is called a "torpedo" line.

Double-taper lines have a thick constant diameter in the middle with thin diameters for several feet at each end. These lines are designed expressly to lay the leader and fly down more softly to impart a more realistic action to the fly.

Most fly lines come in 30- to 35-yard packages and will fit almost every reel.

Where can a beginner learn how to use a fly rod and how to take a fish properly?

There are several fly-fishing schools that are excellent for the beginning angler and where more advanced fly fishermen can also sharpen their skills. Your choice will probably be dictated by the locations and prices of the schools.

The Fenwick Fly Fishing Schools are held in various states during the spring and summer months. Although most are 2-day affairs, they can run to 3, or even 5 days. The Fenwick schools are divided into five regions: Western, Eastern, Midwestern, Montana, and New Mexico. This seems to pretty well blanket the United States (including Alaska) and even reaches into Alberta, Canada. The fees for these 2-day schools vary from $100 to $150. This fee includes the use of Fenwick equipment, some meals, but no lodging. For further details write to

Fenwick
P.O. Box 729
Westminster, Calif. 92683

The H. L. Leonard Rod Company holds 3-day fly-fishing schools at Roscoe, N.Y., in May and June on weekends. The $150 registration fee includes room; meals; tuition; the use of Leonard rods, reels, and lines; and a New York State fishing license. If you desire more information write to

H. L. Leonard Rod Co.
25 Cottage Street
Midland Park, N.J. 07432

The Orvis Fly Fishing Schools are held at Manchester, Vermont, during April, May, June, July, and August. The 3-day sessions cost $195 per person and include lodging, meals, tuition, a tour of the Orvis factory, the use of Orvis fly rods, and a 3-day Vermont fishing license. If you write to the address below, Orvis will be happy to furnish you with additional details.

Orvis Fly Fishing School
10 River Road
Manchester, Vt. 05254

What is meant by the expression "shooting the line"?

This is a fly-casting term for releasing the slack line that was previously stripped from the reel to lengthen the cast. At the proper instant, the momentum of the line being cast will pull the slack line through the guides. This is often done on a back cast, too.

Every year when I ready my tackle and flies for the approaching season, my flies are mashed out of shape. It's rather costly to replace them, and I wonder if there is any practical way that I can salvage them.

You're probably storing too many in your container. When

you compress the flies, they lose their shape. They need plenty of space.

To restore them to their former shapes, place them in a fine-mesh strainer such as a tea strainer and hold them over the steam produced by a kettle of boiling water.

I know that the kinks and curls in my fly line are probably caused by my storing it too long on the reel. What is a good way to eliminate this problem?

Stretch your line for a few minutes. Fasten one end to a stationary object and pull on the other end.

I'm getting a lot of friction and wear on my line knots and guides. How can I overcome this?

Always coat your leader–fly-line knot with a good glue containing a rubber base; a popular brand is Pliobond. After two or three applications, the knot becomes smooth and hard—which eliminates the friction that could cause breakage.

How far can a fly be cast?

This depends upon what kind of fly rod and line you are using. A good dry- or wet-fly fisherman should be able to cast a fly from 100 to 130 feet. Some casts executed by tourney pros measure over 180 feet.

Salmon fly casters who use heavier tackle have been known to cast over 200 feet.

What is meant by "fishing the rise"?

This expression pertains to dry-fly fishing and is generally carried out on smooth water. When trout are jumping and feeding upon the flying insects and those that are fluttering on the surface of the water, an angler will be "fishing the rise."

It is strictly a visual operation. An angler can see where the trout are feeding, what they're feeding on, and where he should present his fly. In other words, there is no guesswork. He is able to identify the insects and match them with his fly patterns.

What is meant by "dimpling"?

When fish are rising to insects and sucking them in with a minimum of disturbance upon the water surface, they are "dimpling" the surface, creating dimples or bubbles on it. These usually indicate that the rise was made by a rather large fish.

What is meant by "false casting"?

The expression pertains to fly casting. "False casting" accomplishes two purposes: one, to dry a fly by casting several times without allowing the fly and line to touch the water, and two, to vary or increase the length of the line.

What is meant by a "Galway cast"?

This is also called a reverse cast. It is a fly cast, bait cast, or spin cast used to avoid obstructions in the rear that may hinder the caster. It begins after the line is raised from the water preparatory to making the back cast, but the angler's body turns to the left or right (whichever he chooses) until he faces in the direction of the back cast, which now becomes a forward cast.

When fishing a stream for trout, how do you determine whether a dry fly or a wet fly is better?

Early in the season or when the water is high and cold, trout will take a wet fly more eagerly than a dry fly. When the water is clear, low, and measuring between 55 and 60 degrees, trout will prefer a dry fly. A positive sign that indicates dry flies should be used is the presence of insects on the water and the appearance of trout rising to them.

How should a dry fly float on top of the water?

As high as possible. Even the hook should not touch the water. A good dry fly, if tied properly with heavy hackle (the long, slender neck and saddle feathers of the prime cock, or rooster), will float high. If it floats low in the water, dip it in dry-fly oil to restore its floating ability.

What is "dapping"?

This is an angling technique using a natural or artificial fly. The fly is touched to the water repeatedly and lifted off immediately, to imitate an insect depositing its eggs. A fairly stout rod is used, since only 3 to 4 feet of leader extends from the rod tip to execute the action—in the usual confines of close quarters.

Why do trout miss my dry fly when I can see them splashing about under a dense swarm of insects hovering only inches above the water?

Take a closer look. Those trout are probably delay-feeding. That is, they're slapping the insects with their tails, swirling about, and then picking up the insects they've stunned. You're anticipating your strike. Try a delayed strike. Leave your fly on the water and strike *only* when you feel the pull, rather than by sight and suspicion.

Where can I get complete instructions on fly tying and purchase good materials?

If you subscribe to any outdoor or fishing periodicals, you can always order books on fly tying from their book clubs. But if you would like personalized instruction, the best place to inquire is at your local fishing clubs. They frequently conduct seminars where you can learn the fine points of fly tying at first hand.

Here are two companies that specialize in selling a complete line of fly-tying materials and tools:

Reed Tackle
P.O. Box 390
Caldwell, N.J. 07006

This company will be happy to send you a free catalog upon request.

Herter's, Inc.
RFD 2, Interstate 90
Mitchell, S.D. 57301

This firm advertises one of the most complete fly-tying dictionaries ever written. Its catalog sells for $1, which will be credited on an order of $10 or more from the company.

I'm rather confused by the different kinds of reels used to catch freshwater fish. Can you give me a brief description of each, and its operation?

Anglers are fortunate indeed to have five basic reels from which to choose. Since each one of them is engineered to catch fish successfully, it is up to the angler to decide the manner in which he wants to catch his quarry.

(1) Spinning is the most popular method of taking fish. It is relatively easy to learn, and the reel is designed to let the angler make long casts with little effort. The reel has an open face and does not revolve. Instead, the line winds, or "spins," on the spool by the action of a component known as the bail. When the reel handle is turned, the bail revolves and places

the line evenly on the spool. For casting, the bail is opened to allow the line to leave the spool with a minimum of drag. After the cast is completed, the first turn of the reel handle (which is synchronized with the spool) locks the bail in place. During the retrieve, the bail automatically guides the line evenly onto the spool.

This reel is manufactured in many sizes, ranging from light to heavy-duty. With a properly matched rod, the angler can troll for large fish, such as muskies and lake trout, or cast for small panfish and bass.

(2) The spin-casting reel is a variation of the spinning reel. The operation of the reel is basically the same except that in place of an open face and bail, a fixed hoodlike housing covers the spool. During a retrieve, an internal component guides the line while it enters an opening in the face of the hood. The reel is equipped with an exterior button or lever that releases the line for casting purposes. During the retrieve, the spool engages automatically and spins the line onto the spool. Spin-casting reels are limited in size and are seldom used to catch large fish.

(3) Bait-casting reels are not as popular as they were before the inception of spinning reels. Although bait-casting reels are manufactured with a drag mechanism, casting is not nearly as easy with them as with a spinning reel. Many anglers choose a bait-casting reel when the situation calls for a stiff rod and heavy line, such as those used to cast heavy plugs or spoons for muskies. Most bait-casting reels have a level-wind mechanism that places the line evenly on the revolving spool. Some anglers use bait-casting gear in addition to other tackle simply because they enjoy diversity in their methods of catching fish.

(4) Fly casting is the oldest (modern-day) method of catching game fish, and it is the most complicated because it requires the most skill and patience. Its popularity stems from the challenge of catching fish with ultralight line and from the skill that the angler must use when he presents his lure to a wary fish.

In fly fishing, as distinguished from other fishing methods, it is the weight of the line that carries the lure to the fish rather than the lure itself. With this kind of tackle, the line is

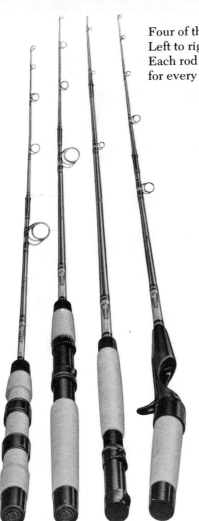

Four of the most popular types of freshwater fishing rods. Left to right: spin-casting, spinning, fly, and bait-casting. Each rod is available in light, medium, and heavy weights for every size of fish. (GARCIA CORP.)

Bait-casting reels are manufactured with drag and level-wind mechanisms. The wide range of models features narrow or wide spools and various speed-of-retrieve ratios. (GARCIA CORP.)

The spinning reel is the most widely used reel in America. Available in a wide range of models, it features different speed-of-retrieve ratios, line-capacity spools, and adjustable drag mechanisms. (THE ORVIS CO.)

Spin-cast reels have a fixed housing covering the line spool, a button at the rear for releasing the line in casting, and a drag mechanism. (GARCIA CORP.)

Fly reels come in various sizes so that anglers can balance their tackle whether they fly-fish for giant muskies or for panfish. (THE ORVIS CO.)

matched to a long, flexible rod. The rod and line together then form a kind of whip that enables the angler to propel a length of light leader and a fly to a desired distance. In this case, the reel functions only as a facility to store the line, since the angler uses his hand to strip line from the reel before making a cast and also while retrieving the line.

(5) Trolling tackle differs from bait-casting gear in two ways: Since heavy equipment is required to catch giant Chinook salmon or to troll deep for big lake trout, both reel and rod are constructed larger. Also, these large trolling reels, designed for either line or wire, lack the level-wind mechanisms normally found on bait-casting reels. The rods are heavier and stiffer—designed and balanced for larger reels carrying heavy line. Obviously, the outfit is too cumbersome for casting.

Can you give me some good pointers on the proper way to use my rod and reel when I'm playing a fish?

I'm sure you realize that entire books have been written on this one subject, so you're probably just looking for a few fundamental techniques and theories, right?

If it were just a question of your strength against the fish's, there would be no art to fishing. Knowledge, practice, and instinct are all-important factors, and each one depends, to a greater or lesser degree, upon the others. Your coordination may be instinctive or developed from practice; your familiarity with your equipment comes through practice and a basic knowledge of the mechanisms involved.

The laws of physics that apply to fishing combine technique, knowledge, and a "feel' that is largely instinctive. To break a fish's spirit (especially a large fish), you must know when to apply line pressure, how long to continue it, and when to relax the pressure as the tension on the line nears the breaking point.

Pressure is controlled by proper adjustment of the reel's drag mechanism. When adjusting the mechanism, you must take into account the extra drag on the reel caused by a bending rod plus the added resistance or friction of the water upon the line. These are some of the finer points that you must consider, especially when you are whipping a large, stubborn fish. If you are to land your fish successfully, you must employ proper techniques even though it involves a lot of wear and tear on muscles and temper.

Remember, your reel has nothing to do with bringing in the fish. It is simply a device that stores your line, geared to a high ratio, and a drag mechanism consisting of many smoothly moving friction clutch plates that will create steady tension while the line is being pulled by a fish. The reel becomes functional only when the fish is exerting pressure on the drag.

An experienced angler not only adjusts his drag mechanism constantly but also applies pressure on the line with his hand to "feel" approximately how close his line is to the breaking point. This gives him a rough idea of how much resistance is required in the drag before he makes his adjustment.

The fish's weight, water resistance, and the added resistance created by the bending rod are the factors that produce pressure on the drag. The resistance, or tension, upon the drag mechanism varies proportionately to the position or bend of the rod. All of these conditions are variables that require quick, accurate estimating by the angler. Only experience can help you to accomplish these feats.

In physics, the law governing pulleys informs us that the tension upon the reel spool and drag increases steadily (while the fish is pulling the line out) as the diameter of the spool becomes smaller. You'd have to be a mathematician to calculate exactly how much tension, in pounds, is created at any given time. But it is a critical factor, and you can expect your line to break if you don't use good judgment in making the correct adjustments while your fish is running off with 75 to 150 feet of line before you can dent his spirit!

Although the angler's strength and stamina are important, the rod actually does the work of bringing in the fish. A major key to skillful angling is in your coordination and timing while you're pumping the rod to pick up the slack line. When to pull up on the rod and when to drop it depend upon the angler's ability to feel the resistance of his fish. The angler must know just how much pressure he can apply to let the fish know who's the master, before the line breaks. An experienced angler tests the breaking limits of his rod and line beforehand. He does this by observing the arc or bend while someone pulls on the line with a scale to measure the maximum tension just before the breaking point occurs.

How do I go about making the correct drag adjustments on my reels?

The breaking point of your line, the amount of line in the water, and the flexibility of your rod are important factors to consider when you're making adjustments in your drag mechanism. Therefore, during the time you're playing a fish you may have to make one, two, or more adjustments. You may have to lighten your drag if your rod is nearing the breaking point, or tighten it if your fish is running too fast. There is really no perfect, single adjustment for all situations.

The accepted rule of thumb to follow is to make a preliminary adjustment before your line hits the water. The drag should be adjusted to about one-third of the line test. In other words, if you are using 12-pound-test line, it should begin to slip off the reel under approximately 4 pounds' pull. This establishes a two-thirds safety margin before the line breaks.

To make accurate adjustments, first place the rod in a fixed position. Then, while pulling the line down (as a fish would), determine the pressure in pounds (or ounces) by using a spring scale attached to the line running off the rod tip. This procedure, called "scaling the line," eliminates a lot of guesswork. After a few practice sessions, you'll be able to make fairly accurate drag adjustments without the use of a scale.

How do I choose the proper tackle for each species?

There *is* no "proper tackle" for each species. The choice is strictly up to you. The main thing is to choose tackle you like and feel comfortable with, so that you can enjoy the use of your equipment. With practice and proper use, you'll eventually become skillful with it.

For example, when a hunter practices shooting clay pigeons, or a golfer spends hours putting and driving, each one is enjoying the use of his equipment *and* honing his skill at the same time.

And so it goes with fishermen. They practice casting to achieve accuracy and effect. This is especially true of fly casters, who practice constantly—knowing that the technique of dropping a dry fly in the most natural manner possible is a pleasurable art in itself. Spin fishermen and bait casters also practice by dropping their lures in difficult targets to achieve casting accuracy.

Obviously, you wouldn't use heavy, bulky gear, such as muskie rods, to catch stream trout. You simply use tackle that is in relative balance with your quarry and is comfortable to handle. Visit a couple of tackle shops and get their version of what balanced tackle means.

I'd like to learn how to build my own fishing rods. Where can I obtain full details and instructions?

There are several large firms that will be glad to send the information you need. Write to

Fenwick
P.O. Box 729
Westminster, Calif. 92683

This company offers a helpful brochure called "Building Fishing Rods" for 25 cents. It contains step-by-step instructions and illustrations showing how to assemble a fly rod, casting rod, trolling rod, or boat rod. If you don't want to start from absolute scratch, the brochure also describes a variety of rod blanks and components that are available.

"Tips on Rod Building" is another instructive booklet that gives all the details for do-it-yourselfers. This booklet is available for $1 from

Gene Bullard Custom Rods, Inc.
10139 Shoreview Road
P.O. Box 38131
Dallas, Tex. 75238

You can get a free catalog including all the materials and component parts for making your own rods from

Reed Tackle
P.O. Box 390
Caldwell, N.J. 07006

or from

Herter's, Inc.
RFD 2, Interstate 90
Mitchell, S.D. 57301

This firm has a giant catalog that includes a wide assortment of component parts for custom-building your own rods. The catalog costs $1, but the price is credited if you order $10 or more from the company.

wick dealer or directly from the factory. For further information, write to

> Fenwick Custom Rod Shop
> Dept. Z
> P.O. Box 729
> Westminster, Calif. 92683

When I make extended fishing trips, I can't fit all my rods into standard cases. What do you suggest I do?

Make one or two custom rod cases from plastic pipe called PVC (polyvinyl chloride). You can cut them to size, cement a plug at one end, and use a screw cover at the other end. This is terrific material and not expensive—compared with the cost of manufactured rod cases. It is corrosion-, water-, and bug-proof, light in weight, and available in colors. (Check your local plumbing-supply house.) The cases you make from it are easy to mount on your car top or camper with tie-down clips, skipper hitches, and snaps.

Is it worthwhile to salvage old scarred and battered plugs?

Definitely, unless you have money to burn! I know many freshwater fishermen are sentimental about some of their favorite plugs and hate to discard them, so they *are* worth salvaging. Besides, it's the practical thing to do. Let's face it, inflation has hit the fishing-tackle business too, and prices for new plugs continue to skyrocket.

Sand off the old faded, chipped paint and repaint or spray with new waterproof paint. Remove the rusty hooks and screw eyes, fill in the holes with epoxy, and insert new ones. The plugs will then be as good as new!

Contrary to popular belief, fish don't hit plugs because they're pretty. It's the action of the plug, plus your ability to manipulate your rod while retrieving, that induces a fish to strike.

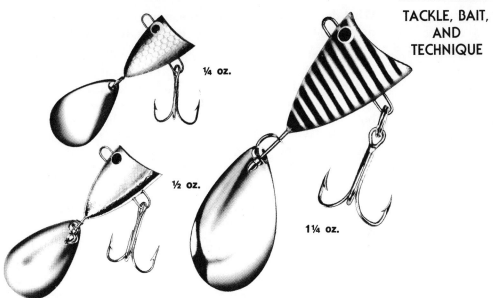

¼ oz.

½ oz.

1¼ oz.

The sound emissions caused by a vibrating spinner blade attract all species of freshwater fish in murky water. In clear water, both the sound *and* the flash of the spinner are attractants. Spinners come in a variety of sizes and can be rigged with live bait or, as shown, with lures. (UNCLE JOSH BAIT CO.)

Why is a spinner so productive in catching fish?

Its sound and appearance are key factors in a spinner's effectiveness. As the spinner revolves, it creates vibration—a sound that is probably very appealing to fish.

Spinners in different sizes attract all kinds of fish from the little sunfishes to the big lake trout and salmon.

They are great to use in streams, where the current helps you to fish them slowly enough to revolve the blades, almost holding the lure in one spot to attract moving fish.

Spinners come in assorted patterns with different shapes and numbers of revolving blades. Some lures are weedless and usually contain two or three blades over a hook buried in a weighted bucktail jig.

What does the word "strike" mean when used in reference to fishing? Do the fish strike or does an angler strike?

They both strike. According to one of Webster's many definitions of the word, strike means "to pull on a fishing rod in order to set the hook," and also *"of a fish:* to seize the bait."

So in angling parlance, the word is used either way, since both fish and angler strike to accomplish their purposes. For example: When a fish strikes to seize a bait, it triggers the angler's reflexes. He, in turn, strikes to hook the fish!

Although anglers will always continue to lose fish, what would you say is the leading cause?

The consensus points to dull hooks as being responsible for the loss of most fish once they strike at a bait. If a hook isn't sharp, chances are the point won't penetrate deep enough for the barb to catch. Since the fish is hooked only temporarily, after a few head-shaking movements or jumps it pulls free.

All anglers, and especially the light-tackle buffs, should keep their hooks extra sharp to make deep penetration easier. When hooks are neglected, line breakage also occurs. Fish are lost because anglers, in their zeal to set the hooks, frequently strike their fish too hard. This often results in ripping the hook out of the fish's mouth or breaking the line.

You'll catch more fish if you keep your hooks sharp! Here's the proper way to use a hook-sharpening stone. A special groove, running the length of the hone, makes the job fast and easy. (THE WORTH CO.)

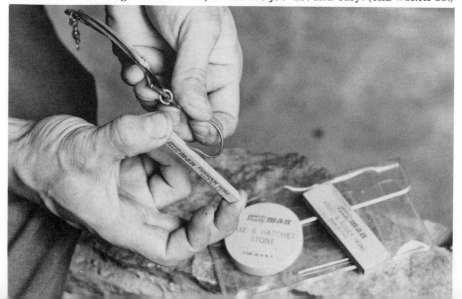

What does "triangulating a hook" mean?

It means filing or honing the point of a hook to create three cutting edges. A cross section of the pointed end would then appear as a triangle.

It has been proved that a hook with cutting edges will penetrate a fish's mouth much quicker and with less effort than a hook with a round point.

Freshwater anglers seldom triangulate their small hooks, since most manufacturers of freshwater gear produce pretty sharp hooks. However, it might be a good idea to triangulate the larger hooks that you use when you're fishing for freshwater species such as muskies, catfish, and sturgeons.

What are some other reasons why anglers lose fish?

Line breakage, due to improperly tied knots, is another major cause of losing fish. This can become rather costly, too, because when a line breaks you lose not only your fish but your terminal tackle as well. Leaders, snaps, swivels, hooks, sinkers, and lures all add up to a pretty piece of change if an angler unknowingly continues to tie a bad knot.

Many anglers are unaware of what actually takes place when a line breaks because of knot failure. One of two things happens: either the knot is tied in such a way that, with pressure, line cuts into line and eventually parts it, or the knot slips. In this case, the line doesn't actually break but the knot simply comes apart. A slight curl at the end of the line is usually a telltale sign that the knot has slipped.

Of course, lines part for other reasons: a heavy fish pulling against a drag that is set too tight; a line that becomes snarled among bottom obstructions. So regardless of how good your knots are, lines will still break occasionally.

A basic knowledge of correctly tied knots, plus proper drag adjustment, will certainly improve an angler's chances for landing bigger fish.

Knots to form double-line leaders—creating a long loop of line that is stronger than the single strand of the standing line. (STREN FISHING LINE)

Spider Hitch

This is a faster, easier knot to create a double-line leader. Under steady pressure it is equally strong but does not have the resilience of the Bimini Twist under sharp impact. Not practical with lines above 30-lb. test

1

Form a loop of the leader length desired. Near the point where it meets the standing line, twist a section into a small reverse loop.

2

Hold small loop between thumb and forefinger with thumb extended well above finger and loop standing out beyond end of thumb.

3

Wind double line around both thumb and loop, taking five turns. Pass remainder of large loop through the smaller one and pull to make five turns unwind off the thumb.

4

Pull turns around the base of the loop up tight and snip off tag end.

Bimini Twist

Measure a little more than twice the footage you'll want for the double-line leader. Bring end back to standing line and hold together. Rotate end of loop 20 times, putting twists in it.

1

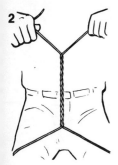

2

Spread loop to force twists together about 10″ below tag end. Step both feet through loop and bring it up around knees so pressure can be placed on column of twists by spreading knees apart.

With twists forced tightly together, hold standing line in one hand with tension just slightly off the vertical position. With other hand, move tag end to position at right angle to twists. Keeping tension on loop with knees, gradually ease tension of tag end so it will roll over the column of twists, beginning just below the upper twist.

3

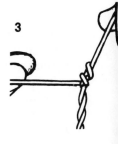

Spread legs apart slowly to maintain pressure on loop. Steer tag end into a tight spiral coil as it continues to roll over twisted line.

4

When spiral of tag end has rolled over column of twists, continue keeping knee pressure on loop and move hand which has held standing line down to grasp knot. Place finger in crotch of line where loop joins knot to prevent slippage of last turn. Take half-hitch with tag end around nearest leg of loop and pull up tight.

5

With half-hitch holding knot, release knee pressure but keep loop stretched out tight. Using remaining tag end, take half-hitch around both legs of loop, but do not pull tight.

6

Make two more turns with the tag end around both legs of the loop, winding inside the bend of line formed by the loose half-hitch and toward the main knot. Pull tag end slowly, forcing the three loops to gather in a spiral.

7

When loops are pulled up neatly against main knot, tighten to lock knot in place. Trim tag end about ¼" from knot.

8

These directions apply to tying double-line leaders of around five feet or less. For longer double-line sections, two people may be required to hold the line and make initial twists.

Knots to tie line to line and line to leader. The two most-often-used knots to join line are the Blood Knot, for two lines of about the same diameter, and the Surgeon's Knot, to join a leader to line when the diameters vary considerably. (STREN FISHING LINE)

Blood Knot

Lay ends of lines alongside each other, lapping about 6" of line. Hold lines at midpoint. Take five turns around standing line with tag end and bring end back between the two strands, where they are being held.

1

Hold this part of the knot in position while the other tag end is wound around the standing line in the opposite direction and also brought back between the strands. The two tag ends should protrude from the knot in opposite directions.

2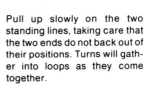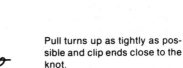

Pull up slowly on the two standing lines, taking care that the two ends do not back out of their positions. Turns will gather into loops as they come together.

3

Pull turns up as tightly as possible and clip ends close to the knot.

4

Surgeon's Knot

Lay line and leader parallel, lapping 6" to 8" of the two strands.

1

Treating the two like a single line, tie an overhand knot, pulling the entire leader through the loop.

2

Leaving loop of the overhand open, pull both tag end of line and leader through again.

3

Hold both lines and both ends to pull the knot tight. Clip ends close to avoid foul-up in rod guides.

4

Knots to hold terminal tackle—vital connections between line, hook, and lure or special rig. (STREN FISHING LINE)

Improved Clinch Knot

An old standby. Pass line through eye of hook, swivel or lure. Double back and make five turns around the standing line. Hold coils in place; thread end of line through first loop above the eye, then through big loop, as shown.

Hold tag end and standing line while coils are pulled up. Take care that coils are in spiral, not lapping over each other. Slide tight against eye. Clip tag end.

Palomar Knot

Easier to tie right, and consistently the strongest knot known to hold terminal tackle. Double about 4″ of line and pass loop through eye.

Pull loop of line far enough to pass it over hook, swivel or lure. Make sure loop passes completely over this attachment.

Let hook hang loose and tie overhand knot in doubled line. Avoid twisting the lines and don't tighten knot.

Pull both tag end and standing line to tighten. Clip about ⅛″ from knot.

Snelling a Hook

Using this common snell, hook and leader combinations can be made up to suit the length and strength needed for various types of fishing.

Move fingers to hold coils tightly in place. Pull leader extending from eye until entire loop has passed under coils.

Insert one end of leader material through eye of hook just past turn and barb. Pass other end through eye in opposite direction, leaving large loop hanging down.

With coils snugged up neatly, use pliers to pull tag end, cinching up snell. Clip off tag end and tie loop knot in end of leader.

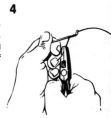

Hold both lines along shank. Use line hanging from eye to wind tight coils around shank and both lines from eye toward hook. Take 5 to 10 turns.

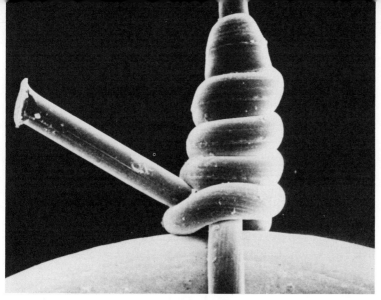

Here's a classic example of a properly tied Improved Clinch Knot—
photographed at many times natural size through a scanning electron
microscope used to examine monofilament line. Note how the pre-
scribed five turns cushion the line and protect against breakage in
the knot. (STREN FISHING LINE)

Is there any kind of knot-tying device on the market?

Yes, you're in luck. Check with your tackle shop for Sports
Liquidator's new fishhook sneller and "knot tier."

The gadget makes it easy to tie Clinch Knots, Barrel Knots,
Blood Knots, Drop Loops, and End Loops. You can also use it
to splice line and to make tapered leaders.

**Now that my eyesight is failing, I'm having trouble tying lead-
ers to hooks. Do you have any suggestions?**

There's an old hook-threading trick, probably conceived by
a night fisherman, that can be used by those with poor eyesight during the day, too. With the tip of your tongue as a
guide, place the eye of the hook sideways on your tongue.
Then, holding only an inch or so of your leader, while brush-
ing the end against your tongue, try to thread the eye. You'll
be surprised how easily this is done, since you can feel when
the leader is in its proper position going through the hook's
eye.

How does "keeping a tight line" reduce the chances of losing a fish?

It doesn't always work, especially when you're using light tackle or a fly rod for salmon, trout, or bass. These natural acrobats head for the sky when they feel sudden resistance against their movements, or the sting of a hook. Their gyrations either create slack or put undue strain upon the line or hook. The line can part or the hook can pull out. So when your fish leaps, you must create slack by lowering your rod tip to release the pressure. However, while the fish is *in* the water, you should maintain a "tight line," except for the line under tension that leaves the spool of a properly adjusted reel.

When a fish jumps, drop your rod to give your line slack. Otherwise, the sudden stress will pop the line or pull out the hook. The explosive leap of this smallmouth caused the plastic worm to blur—even when photographed at 1/1,000 of a second! (HAL SCHARP)

I favor my ten-pound spinning outfit for most fishing, but I've been losing big fish lately from line breakage. Even replacing line doesn't solve the problem. Any suggestions?

Well, we'll discount original line flaw, since you've been replacing your line. However, flaws or defects can develop in new line after you install it on your reel, for a number of reasons.

First, make a close examination of your rod guides and tip—with a strong magnifying glass. A rough burr at any of these places can be enough to fray and weaken your line. If in doubt, replace the guides.

If your rod is okay, consider your knot style next. You may be using an incorrect knot for tying monofilament. Try switching to a knot such as the Improved Clinch Knot, which prevents slippage and minimizes the chances of a knot's breaking.

Check your bail roller. The surface should be perfectly smooth and snug against its housing, but free enough to revolve while the line is pulled off the spool. A small nick or burr at this location can fray your line in no time. Don't try to smooth over a defect by sanding or filing. This metal is mirror-smooth and extra hard. Only the factory or a good repair shop can give it the required frictionproof surface. For the cost involved, I wouldn't fool with it. I would just replace the roller and/or bail with a new one.

One major culprit that causes line breakage is sticky spool drag. Regardless of the great elastic qualities in monofilament line, when a strong acrobatic fish puts sudden pressure on the spool and it doesn't respond quickly, the line will break. Check your drag frequently, at different settings. If you find it a little sticky at one or more positions, the entire drag assembly should be cleaned and lubricated.

If your problem still persists, examine the spool and drag components. If any are defective or questionable, replace the entire drag assembly or spool.

I often hear fishermen talking about "line fatigue." What does this mean, and what causes it?

This usually occurs with lines made of plastic material called monofilament, or "mono." A mono line is "fatigued" when its strength begins to diminish for reasons other than the wear caused by friction or nicks.

There are two major factors that cause fatigue. Heat, which is particularly damaging, comes from constant exposure to direct sunlight. Some lines may even become dry or brittle. Hard use (from catching too many heavy fish) will also break down a line's efficiency by stretching it too often. A combination of the two factors is usually the direct cause of lines' wearing out prematurely.

With new technological advances in the manufacture of mono, some premium lines have been developed that resist the ultraviolet rays of the sun and thus have a longer life expectancy.

From the standpoint of physics, think of mono line as a rubber band. Constant stretching will eventually break it. Leave it out in the sun and it will dry out, become brittle, and deteriorate. When the line loses its limpness and becomes hard, or a slight change in color occurs, the line should be replaced. This will give you maximum insurance against breakage.

How can I limber up stiffly coiled monofilament line before putting it on a reel?

Play the line out into the wake of your boat—increasing your speed a little to stretch the line just enough to remove the coils. Be sure to slow down before putting the line on the reel. If it goes on too tight, it may explode the spool or the line will stretch enough to create new coils.

I've heard anglers say that monofilament line has "memory." What is meant by this expression?

"Memory" simply means that monofilament line has a tendency to return to its original storage position. This memory causes the line to coil when it leaves the spool after it has been stored under tension for some time.

When I'm using an open-face spinning reel, my monofilament line occasionally develops a twist after a day of fishing. What causes this, and how can I prevent it?

A twist is often caused by a defective swivel. If you're using a revolving lure and the swivel doesn't function properly, your line will become twisted. The same thing happens if you continue to reel while your drag mechanism is slipping. This usually occurs when you're fast to a fish or when your bait is snagged. Don't forget, each revolution of the reel head (while your line is stationary) is equal to the ratio of the reel handle to the reel head. For example, with a 3½:1 reel, one complete turn of the reel handle will cause the reel head to make 3½ revolutions.

If you're catching a lot of fish by trolling or casting, naturally your line is bound to develop a little twist—even with good working swivels. If the twist constitutes a problem, it's a good idea to remove the terminal tackle and play the line out into the wake of the boat. In minutes, the line will straighten out and you're back in business. If you can't use a boat, lay the working portion of your line on your lawn, secure the free end to the chuck of a hand drill, and wind away. Be sure you know in which direction you must wind to remove the twist, and watch for anything on the lawn that may damage your line.

What causes the tangled line in a bait-casting reel?

A "bird's nest," or snarl, is caused when a forward cast is suddenly terminated and the spool revolves faster than the pull of the line. This, in turn, causes the spool to overrun with loose line.

Since fish also rely upon their hearing to locate food, is there any sound-producing device that I can use to increase the attraction of my bait?

Try the "Rattler" lure made by the Little Beaver Manufacturing Co. This is a simple little plastic capsule containing three or four small steel balls. Slight movement causes the balls to rattle and emit a vibration in the water that attracts the attention of fish. The capsules can be inserted into plastic worms or glued to plugs, spoons, bucktails, or any other lure or bait.

In this age of computers, hasn't anyone come up with some kind of device that will do the thinking for any angler and help put him onto fish right away?

Well, not exactly—except for fish-finding instruments. However, there *is* a device called the Lowrance Fishing Calculator. With a turn of the dial, you find a short biography of the fish, preferred temperatures, best baits, optimum spawning temperatures, and world's-record weights. You can also match specific bottom and cover characteristics with corresponding signals transmitted by all Lowrance Locator/Sounders. The calculator sells for $1 and can be ordered from
Lowrance Electronics, Inc.
12000 E. Skelly Drive
Tulsa, Okla. 74128

I'm planning to buy an electronic fish-finding instrument, but I'm confused by all the different models. What kind of unit do you recommend for fishing in lakes no deeper than 150 feet?

Practically all fish-finders are based on the principle of

Every serious angler who fishes from a boat knows the value of fish-finding equipment. This unit, a combination flasher and recorder, enables anglers to locate schools of fish and to identify bottom characteristics. (LOWRANCE ELECTRONICS)

"sonar" (an abbreviation of "sound, navigation, and ranging"). This system was developed as a means of tracking enemy submarines during World War II.

There are two types produced that would be practical for your use. One model, sometimes called a "blip" or "flasher," offers a quick reading. The other is a combination flasher and recorder that gives you a reading on graph paper and provides you with a permanent record of your "contacts." The latter is a more sophisticated instrument which costs approximately twice as much (starting at about $200) as the flasher.

If you are a serious fisherman, you should spend the extra money and go for the recorder. This unit gives you a clear outline of bottom contours and the visual location of fish between your boat and the bottom. It's easier to read and fun to use. Expert anglers wouldn't fish without a recorder—knowing that their productivity is increased tremendously.

Is it possible to build my own electronic fish-finding equipment? If so, where can I obtain a kit?

For details and models offered, write for the catalog of
  Heath Co.
  Benton Harbor, Mich. 49022
This company sells fish-finders, spotters, and thermometers in kit form so that you can assemble your own units.

Is a thermometer an essential part of an angler's equipment? If so, how does he use it correctly?

Definitely. A thermometer can be one of the most important tools in an angler's tackle box. However, it should be pointed out that only the expensive electronic models are accurate and can read the temperatures at any depth within seconds. There are other, nonelectronic models that are less costly, but more time is required to obtain fairly accurate readings with them.

As an electronic model is being lowered, it gives you the readings and depths at the same time. The nonelectronic model consists of a container that opens to let water in at any level. The sample is pulled up immediately and the angler takes a reading by holding a regular thermometer in it. Readings should be taken at 5- or 6-foot intervals until the right level is found. Theoretically, the fish should be where the temperature is correct, and you should begin fishing at that depth.

Are these new temperature meters practical, and how do they work?

Some anglers swear by them and wouldn't be without one. The electronic thermometers are useful only if you're knowledgeable about the temperature comfort range of your quarry. Then you simply drop your probe over the side and read the temperatures right there in your boat. If you know that your fish requires a range of temperature between 67 and 75 degrees F., then you'll know at what depth the fish are likely to be found. With a temperature meter, you can become more selective with your strategy once you learn which species prefer which comfort ranges.

Do oxygen meters have any merit?

Yes, they're quite effective. Since it's a known fact that fish require oxygen to survive, they will, naturally, seek waters with a comfortable oxygen content. For example, bass are normally found in a range of 5 to 13 ppm (parts per million) of oxygen in the water. Because oxygen content and temperatures are so closely related, some manufacturers have made units that combine both meters. With one probe, you can receive a direct readout of water temperature *and* oxygen content!

Since saltwater fishermen use chum to attract fish, why can't I do the same thing with freshwater fish?

You might be able to chum freshwater fish—in some instances. However, you'd better check local and state regulations first, to see if this practice is permitted. Since some states prohibit even the use of mechanical propulsion in trolling for fish, they *might* be a little sticky about using chum.

Chumming is more successful in salt water because of the existing currents. Particles of food that are carried by the currents will attract fish from considerable distances. With little or no movement of the water in lake fishing, chumming will not be as effective. But a handful of cut-up worms, minnows, or terrestrial insects scattered over the water occasionally will certainly keep a school of fish interested enough to stick close to your boat.

However, if some water movement or current exists and you don't mind the mess and a little effort, you'll improve your catches by using homemade chum. Just use the ingredients that make up the diet of the fish you want to catch. For example, walleyes like all sorts of small fish, especially mudminnows and chubs. Grind them up with dog chow (puppy diet) to make a fifty–fifty mixture. Then add cod-liver oil (about 2 ounces to a pound) and refrigerate. Empty quart milk cartons are excellent for storing this gruel.

Naturally, you'll chum only while you're still-fishing at anchor. Don't forget that overchumming your fish satisfies their appetites and discourages them from taking a baited hook. So you don't need much—just enough to get a fish excited and less cautious.

To disperse the chum, you can use a ladle or fill a fine-mesh bag with chum and hang it over the side of your boat. Jiggle the bag occasionally to allow the particles to flow from the bag.

Every time I get a strike I waste valuable time snatching the rod out of the holder to set the hook. Isn't there some device on the market that is more efficient?

You're in luck! Check with your local tackle shop for the new Tempo rod holder. Easily mounted on almost any vertical surface, and adjustable to three different positions, it allows you to set your hook quickly without removing your rod from the holder. It also features an exclusive "drop-back" ring that holds your rod in an upright position—leaving both your hands free to bait your hook.

Now a fisherman can save precious time in setting the hooks into his fish without removing his rod from the holder. Right, the "drop-back" ring allows the angler to use both hands to bait his hook. (TEMPO PRODUCTS)

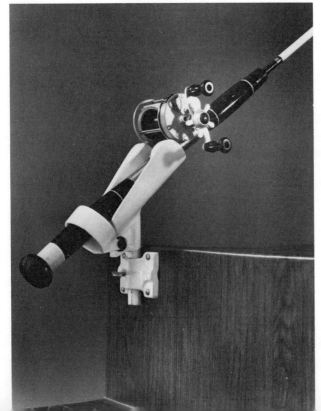
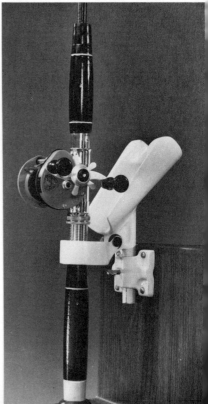

When bowfishing in the spring, look for carp spawning in shallow, muddy water. Not only is it great sport, but you'll help exterminate a scavenger that causes great damage to the ecosystem of game fish. (BEAR ARCHERY CO.)

How does bowfishing work, and what are its advantages?

Bowfishing requires a strong bow—one that will pull 30 pounds or more. If you're shooting sharks, you'll need at least a 50-pound bow to penetrate their tough skins.

A simple snap-on–type spinning reel or one that can be taped to the bow is used. For heavy game, 25 yards of 90-pound-test braided nylon line is adequate. For smaller game, 50 feet of 60- or 70-pound-test line can be used.

Arrows with permanent barbed points or interchangeable points are available. Some points are retractable, with a movable barb for easy removal.

Bowfishing can be a very satisfying sport—one that offers a challenge especially when you're shooting heavy alligator gars, large sharks, or stingrays that are found in the shallows of our coastlines.

Archers find bowfishing an excellent diversion. They can keep in practice when most game is out of season. Anglers too enjoy bowfishing when the season is closed on protected species. The extermination of trash fish such as carp, buffalo, gars, etc. which are usually detrimental to a lake's ecology ensures the survival of many game species.

TACKLE, BAIT, AND TECHNIQUE

What is the difference between mudminnows and mud puppies? Are they both good bait?

Mudminnows are small, dark baitfish that are found in northern lakes and rivers. They are especially good bait because they are hardy and frisky, require little oxygen, and are able to remain alive for a considerable time with a hook impaled in their backs.

Mud puppies are salamanders—scaleless, lizardlike amphibians. They are sometimes called water dogs because the large ones can bite. Although mud puppies are rather ugly-looking, they are not poisonous. They are excellent bait for the bass that inhabit the waters of the western and southwestern United States.

What are "garden hackles"?

They are angleworms. The expression is often used by anglers who frown upon the use of worms or other live bait to take fish.

Healthy garden hackles (worms), surefire bait for almost any freshwater fish, keep well in Styrofoam containers filled with worm bedding. When fed bits of Kraft paper or soft cardboard and refrigerated, they'll live for many weeks. (HAL SCHARP)

During the spring and fall, an inlet to a lake or pond is a productive place to fish because the flowing water carries a constant supply of food to the waiting fish. (GEORGIA NATURAL RESOURCES DEPT.)

What clues should I look for when I try my luck on a strange lake?

If it is a large lake with plenty of fish, boat liveries or bait shops are excellent sources of information. Proprietors like to see their customers return for repeat business and are usually willing to pass on a few closely guarded secrets.

But there's more to it than that. Fish are continually on the move—either prowling for food or seeking comfort and safety. Their movements and feeding habits are governed by many factors, such as the time of year, time of day, water temperature, wind direction, barometric pressure, condition of the water, etc.

You have to familiarize yourself with the lake and try different locations—spots that attract fish and are logically related to the lake's physical characteristics. This means looking for deep water, shallow water, sandbars, rocky bottoms, weed beds, and stream inlets. Fish can be spawning, feeding, or just skulking in the cool depths during the hot summer months.

Sounding with a lead line will find the deeper areas in the lake. Watch for changes in water color. Dark water suggests deeper areas, while light water indicates shallow or sandy bottoms. Steep cliffs indicate deep water near the shoreline. A projection of land or a point usually extends underwater and serves as a sandbar. Caves and grassy areas are good in the early-morning and evening hours. Stream inlets are excellent grounds, since all sorts of aquatic organisms, small fish, worms, and insects caught in the current will eventually be deposited in the lake at the mouth. Fish are naturally attracted to a food source such as this.

If the water is relatively clear, you might use a glass-bottomed bucket or a diving mask and look for irregularities in the bottom contour. Depressions, holes, and rocky bottoms are good holding places for fish.

After I find a good fishing spot far out on a lake, what can I do to be sure of finding it again?

There are two methods: by triangulation or by compass bearings. Using triangulation, find two objects (one behind the other) that will be in line. Then line up two objects on another shore (preferably at a right angle), making your position the intersection of the two lines. Some anglers take photographs or make sketches of these bearings for future use.

If the objects are obscure because of distance, you can use a compass to pick out single objects or bearings. Using a compass is tricky and takes more time, but it is just as accurate when care is taken in reading the relative bearings.

Where can I obtain some movies on sport fishing to show at our club meetings?

Write to
  Fishing Information Bureau
  20 North Wacker Drive
  Chicago, Ill. 60606

Or to
    Boyd Film Company
    1569 Selby Avenue
    St. Paul, Minn. 55104

The bottom of a lake where I fish is congested with a lot of tree stumps, branches, and heavy grass. I lose many deep-running lures and wonder if there is some kind of gadget that will retrieve a snagged lure.

An ingenious device called "Snagaway" can be purchased at leading sporting-good stores. The gadget slides over your line and goes down to the lure, slides over it and, at a tug of the braided nylon line in your other hand, exerts a grip on the hook and releases your lure. It retails for about $7 and will certainly pay for itself after several recoveries.

What are "float trips"?

"Float trips" are fishing trips made in substantial, flat-bot-

Float-trip safaris, utilizing flat-bottomed boats and rubber rafts, are gaining in popularity because they are an exciting, and productive, way of fishing wilderness streams.

tomed craft. The angler floats downstream and casts over likely spots on the way. There's no turning back upstream to fish an area again because of the difficulty of maneuvering the boat in the current. Sometimes professional guides are available on these trips.

When I'm stream-fishing, I lose a lot of fish while attempting to net them. They flop a couple of times on the edge of the net, and off they go! What am I doing wrong?

It sounds as if you're trying to lift them into your net instead of scooping them up. If you have any physical ailments, such as back and knee problems, they could restrict your form and prevent you from reaching out farther and deeper with your net.

Try practicing with a water-soaked rag on the end of your line. If you have trouble slipping your net under it while reaching out, give more length to your line and pull your rod farther back behind you.

Isn't luck the biggest factor in catching a lot of fish?

I'd like to say yes—just to make you feel better about all those times you came home "skunked"; but I can't. Luck is just about the *least* important factor in catching fish.

Successful anglers (the 5 percent who catch 95 percent of the fish) work hard to achieve success. They know that preparation is the name of the game. Besides knowing the water condition and the fish's feeding habits, they must also choose the correct tackle and the right baits or lures. That's what separates the experts from the "also-rans"!

What is meant by "noodling" or "cuddling"?

These expressions refer to a technique used by courageous fishermen who, without the benefit of fishing gear, capture fish by hand. A fish, such as a large catfish, is approached quietly by the fisherman, who lulls it into a sleeplike trance by stroking its belly gently with his fingers. Before the fish can regain its senses, it is lifted quickly from the water and thrown upon the bank. It's rather a dangerous business, since a large fish may bite when it is removed from the water.

Although noodling, or cuddling, is a primitive technique, it is still practiced all over the world.

Now and then I hear the expression "skittering." What kind of fishing is this?

Skittering, as Webster defines it, means "to draw the hook through or along the surface of the water with a twitching or quivering motion."

This is done with a long cane pole and a line baited with a strip of fish belly, pork chunk, or spinner. This kind of fishing was practiced widely before fly fishing and bait and spin casting became so popular.

Actually, it is still practiced in a nonsporting way by the commercial tuna fishermen, who use a heavier pole and line while fishing from the railing of a tuna clipper far out in the ocean in the midst of a dense school of feeding tuna.

How many species of mayflies are there, and what are their stream mannerisms?

There are over 500 species of mayflies throughout the world. In their larval stage (nymph) they are divided into four types: swimmer, clamberer, clinger, and burrower. Each type eventually rises from the stream bottom to shed its shuck before becoming a dun fly in maturity.

When I'm using assorted baits such as grasshoppers, minnows, and worms, shouldn't the point of the hook be buried in the bait so that the fish can't see it?

Not necessarily. It has been proved many times, especially in fly fishing, that the point of a hook does not cause fish to become suspicious. Since fish see all sorts of objects in the water, an exposed hook can very well appear as a twig held by the bait. As a rule, leaving the hook exposed is more likely to increase the chances of hooking your fish.

I usually have good luck catching bass and panfish by using live insects and allowing them to float on the surface. But on windy days, my casts fall short. Any suggestions?

You need a little weight to get out farther, but you don't want your bait to sink. Here's an old trick that always works. Tie a couple of candy Life Savers or a lump of sugar about 12 inches from your bait. It will sink a few feet, but in a few minutes, when the candy dissolves, your bait will swim up to the surface and give you the natural action fish can't resist.

Where can an arm amputee purchase a device that will enable him to use a rod and reel?

I would advise him to contact
   Mr. Roy Dodgen
   Blue Eye, Mo. 65611
Mr. Dodgen manufactures a device called the "Spare Hand Fishing Belt." The belt is lightweight and about four inches in width. I'm assuming that the angler has one good hand and arm that he can use for casting. He can fish with either a fly or a spinning rod.

After he casts in the normal matter, he engages the hollow rod handle on a ratcheted prong that protrudes from the belt. When he turns the rod loose, an automatic mechanism in the handle locks and holds the rod securely in any position while the bait is worked or the fish is played.

As a bonus, a small vise mounted on the belt permits the angler to tie a fly or thread a hook on the line.

I would like to purchase maps of some of the reservoirs in our country where fishing is reportedly good. How do I go about buying them?

You have to order the maps, and that requires three letters. Before you order, you must have a map number. For that, write to Map Information Office, Reston, Va. 22092. Describe the exact location, and specify that you want a map for fishing purposes and need depth information. The office will send you the number. Now you'll need some order forms to acquire the maps. These can be obtained from either the U.S. Geological Survey or the U.S. Corps of Engineers, Washington, D.C.

If the reservoirs are east of the Mississippi River, send the numbers and order forms to Distribution Section, Geological Survey, 1200 South Eads Street, Arlington, Va. 22202.

If the locations are west of the Mississippi, write to Distribution Section, Geological Survey, Federal Center, Denver, Colo. 80225.

I'm planning a long fly-in trip into several wilderness lakes. Since space and weight are important considerations, how can I avoid carrying bulky tackle boxes?

Have you thought of wearing a tackle jacket? Some models of this light, warm garment feature as many as twenty different-sized compartments to store your equipment. These jackets are also ideal for portaging from one lake to another.

Since weight and space are serious considerations when you're flying into wilderness lakes, a warm tackle jacket is mighty practical for carrying your gear. The big northern was taken in north Quebec. (QUEBEC TOURIST BRANCH)

TACKLE, BAIT, AND TECHNIQUE

Where can I find complete details on fishing in Alaska?

Write to
Alaska Dept. of Fish and Game
Information and Education Section
Subport Building
Juneau, Alaska 99801

Ask for a copy of "Alaska Sport Fishing Guide." This booklet contains all the current angling information on fishing locations accessible from the highways and also information on fly-in waters. It lists the cities and villages where air or boat charter service is available. In addition, this guide has many maps that pinpoint the fishing spots and lists the kinds of fish found in each.

I'd like to introduce sport fishing to my nine-year-old son. What's the best way to begin?

It's only natural for your son to emulate you, so you must remember to stress good sportsmanship and conservation

Don't practice false economy! Give your youngster good-quality fishing equipment, but also teach him the proper way to use and care for it. Your relationship will become more meaningful, and you'll acquire a terrific fishing partner! (EVINRUDE MOTORS)

practices. Try to promote his curiosity; dissect a fish occasionally, examine its stomach contents, and explain their relation to artificial lures. Most youngsters are interested in fish biology and aquariums, so it might be a good idea to raise a few panfish.

Find some children's adventure books about fishing (not too technical). The typical "Me 'n Joe" stories are good for him to read.

Don't purchase cheap tackle just because he'll outgrow it or damage it. Tackle doesn't have to be expensive, but it should be substantial so that it's less likely to break down. Don't forget, he can become exasperated with inferior gear, just as you do. Teach him how to give his equipment good care so that he can be proud of his ability to use and maintain it.

Answer all his questions, including those which you might believe are silly and unrelated. If you're not able to answer any of his questions, admit it, but tell him that you'll find the answer. Children have uncanny perception regarding an adult's attitude, so don't try to double-talk or outfox him when he makes inquiries. Above all, be completely honest with him and practice absolute patience. You are fortunate in having a son who provides you with a wonderful challenge. Fishing will help mold his character—provided you apply yourself in his behalf. A father and son fishing and learning together can be a beautiful relationship. Your reward? The best fishing partner ever!

PART THREE

Science and the Angler

———

I'm a staunch advocate of the preservation of wildlife. I would like to participate in some kind of fishing or hunting that will not destroy game. Any suggestions?

Unfortunately, if you hunt you must score a kill in order to capture your game. Many hunters have changed their ideologies and now shoot their game with cameras.

Fishing might be your best bet if you're not interested in "shutter shooting." When you hook a fish and land it, the capture is accomplished and your goal is achieved. Then you can release your fish so that it can be caught and fight another time. Nine times out of ten, the average fish is *not* mortally hooked. So you are practicing good sportsmanship and contributing to the perpetuation of the species.

If the fish is large and you wish to land it without injury, and recover your hook, a small barbless hand gaff can be used. The gaff is thrust into the mouth and through the lower jaw. Only a small area of membrane will be damaged, with little or no bleeding. In this way you have good control of the fish's head, making it easier to remove the hook.

Some anglers fish with barbless hooks. If these cannot be acquired, it takes only a few minutes to file the barbs off. After a fish is played and brought alongside (a very skillful maneuver indeed!), the fish is given slack line and allowed to flop off the hook.

Most anglers who practice release methods simply sever the leader at a point closest to the hook, releasing the fish with the hook intact. It is common knowledge that because of a fish's chemical makeup, the hooks will disintegrate in a short time and cause no harm to the fish.

Isn't spearfishing contributing to the fast depletion of game and food fishes?

No, not really. Legislative controls are pretty strong along the United States coasts. Actually, in some areas, bans have been lifted since detailed investigations and accurate analyses have shown that spearfishermen don't take as many fish as the conservationists feared.

In some instances along the coasts, special areas have been legalized specifically for spearfishing. Naturally, it is illegal to spearfish along beaches used by swimmers, and this is enforced by local ordinances. A high-powered speargun is a dangerous weapon and should not be used in areas where people congregate.

I would like to read more about the habits of fishes, conservation, and ecology. Can you recommend several good books?

The following books will offer authoritative and in-depth information on those subjects:

> *Ichthyology:* The Study of Fishes by Lagler, Bardach, and Miller. (New York: John Wiley & Sons, Inc.)
>
> *McClane's Standard Fishing Encyclopedia* by 141 authorities. (New York: Holt, Rinehart & Winston)
>
> *The Ways of Fishes* by Leonard P. Schultz. (New York: D. Van Nostrand Co.)

The Fresh-Water Fisherman's Bible by Vlad Evanoff.
(New York: Doubleday & Company, Inc.)
Through the Fish's Eye by Mark Sosin. (New York: Harper & Row)

SCIENCE AND
THE ANGLER

What are some of the pollutants that affect or destroy fish and their related life supports? What causes this pollution?

Insecticides, oil spills, plastic and synthetic fibers, soaps and detergents, radioactive wastes, fertilizers, pulp-mill wastes, hot and cold water discharged by factories, and silt caused by dredging operations are all forms of pollution.

Agricultural chemicals contribute to pollution by natural runoff into streams, rivers, and lakes. Industrial and municipal wastes that are improperly treated are poured into rivers by direct methods. Radioactive pollution may be caused by direct fallout or by discharges from nuclear power plants into adjacent streams.

Why do fish in our lakes and streams suddenly die, for no apparent reason, during the hot summer months?

There are any number of reasons why a sudden "fish kill" takes place during the summer. Barring chemicals and industrial wastes, pollution from decaying vegetation is one of the major causes of sudden death for a great number of fish. Unfortunately, this is a natural phenomenon for which only nature can be blamed.

Large concentrations of plankton (in highly fertile waters) require sunlight to thrive. Therefore, a succession of hot, cloudy days will kill off plant organisms. In the process of decomposition, dead plankton consume large amounts of oxygen in the water, leaving little or none for fish to breathe. Eventually, fish will suffocate from the scarcity of oxygen. When you see fish at the surface gulping air, this usually signals the beginning of a fish kill.

187

How much oxygen do fish require to sustain life?

Generally, fish require at least 4 or 5 parts of dissolved oxygen per 1,000,000 parts of water. In some instances, however, depending upon the species and its metabolism, some have been known to survive in a much lower concentration of dissolved oxygen.

Is it true that some insecticides used on a farm can kill fish in a lake 20 miles away?

Yes. During the rainy season fertilizers, insecticides, and fungicides are carried by runoff into streams that lead into the lake. These poisons eventually become so concentrated that they cause a change in the life-support system of the lake's inhabitants.

Research studies reveal that in some cases, fish are affected genetically by poisonous transmissions traced to a source hundreds of miles away!

What organization can I join to help combat pollution in our lakes and streams?

The Izaak Walton League of America. Backed by a membership of over fifty thousand, this organization has been instrumental in combating pollution and in restoring our forest, soil, and water resources. It frequently joins with other conservation groups, at both local and national levels, to fight any threats to our environment.

To find out more about its aims and goals, write to
Izaak Walton League of America
1800 N. Kent Street
Arlington, Va. 22209

How can fishing clubs help guarantee that sport fishing will continue to grow and be productive?

There are many measures that sport-fishing organizations

can initiate to encourage the conservation, restoration, and perpetuation of game fishes. They can work closely with their state conservation commissions or fish-and-wildlife agencies by submitting proposals for artificial reefs and by reporting pollution and fish kills; cooperate with state marine biologists in group or individual capacities by submitting atypical specimens indicating physiological changes and unnatural behavior of fish; keep members advised of all bills dealing with sport fishing that come before their state legislatures, and increase membership to establish stronger representation; establish or promote some kind of educational program about marine ecology with emphasis on the significant part that related creatures (such as those found in the food chain) play in the perpetuation of game fishes.

What does the U.S. Government do in the interest of sport fishing in this country?

In addition to the work being done by the Fish and Wildlife Service of the U.S. Department of the Interior, special legislation has been enacted for the benefit of anglers. A law called the Dingell-Johnson Act was passed by Congress in 1950 to improve sport-fishing facilities in the United States, Puerto Rico, the Virgin Islands, and Guam. Funds are allocated to improve fishery-management programs based upon the number of anglers and the land area of each state. The angler, whose fishing tackle and gear are taxed under the federal excise-tax regulations, indirectly supports the cost of the program.

Provisions of the Dingell-Johnson Act are administered by the Bureau of Sport Fisheries and Wildlife, which distributes funds to the state agencies for fishery research, improvement of fish environments, purchases of land and waters, construction of facilities, and other related fishery-management activities. The state is allowed to select and develop the project that will most benefit its own sport fishing.

What is the Bureau of Sport Fisheries and Wildlife, and what is its function?

The bureau is an agency of the U.S. Department of the Interior. It operates national fish hatcheries and national wildlife refuges, controls predatory animals, enforces federal laws pertaining to fish and wildlife, and engages in research and related activities. The bureau's primary objective is to provide and ensure recreation for the public.

What kind of policy governs the distribution of trout from the national fish hatcheries?

The stocking policy (from circular R P-57, U. S. Department of the Interior, Bureau of Sport Fisheries and Wildlife) is as follows:

     1. Primary obligation will be in the stocking of waters on Federal lands or waters in which the Federal Government has an interest. These waters include lakes, ponds,

Hatchery personnel herding trout for breeding purposes. The attendant in center, front, is using an electroshocker to stun the fish momentarily so that they can be netted. (MONTANA FISH & GAME)

and streams in National Forests, National Parks, Indian reservations, military reservations, and others that are open to public fishing.

2. Secondary obligation will be in the stocking of State waters which are open to the public. These include lakes, ponds, and streams in State management areas and others.

3. If any fish remain after the above obligations are met, they may be planted in private uncommercialized water.

The demand for hatchery trout for public fishing waters usually far exceeds the supply. Fish produced at national fish hatcheries are allocated to areas where the greatest public benefit will be realized.

Whenever possible, trout from a national fish hatchery are stocked only after studies by fishery biologists show the suitability of the water concerned and the species, size, and number of fish needed to produce a high level of angler success.

What do you suppose causes a good trout stream to convert into a bass stream?

There are several causes. The accidental stocking of bass in trout waters will soon bring about a decline in the trout population. The more predaceous bass will feed upon the small trout and eventually replace them.

Bass are able to survive under conditions that are detrimental to trout, such as the physical changes that occur in a stream and its embankment. During the course of lumbering operations, the removal of shoreline trees and the resulting elimination of shade makes the water too warm for trout. Logjams, causing a decrease in water flow and a rise in temperature, will also make a stream unsuitable for trout.

Do artificially bred trout grow faster than those growing in their natural habitats? If so, why?

Artificially bred trout reach greater proportions more

quickly because they are fed a balanced diet on a regular schedule under excellent climatic conditions.

The two most important factors governing the growth of fish are food and water temperature. Of course, when ideal temperatures and food supplies are present, trout will thrive and become larger than those in areas where conditions are not as good.

Exactly what does a state do with the money I spend for my fishing license?

These funds are allotted to many departments concerned with improving fishing conditions and perpetuating the species indigenous to your state. The money is used for administration, operation of state hatcheries, conservation, regulation enforcement, and research.

The money you spend for a fishing license is returned to the lakes and streams in the form of healthy fingerling trout. (WISCONSIN NATURAL RESOURCES DEPT.)

How do biologists determine the number of fish in a given stream? Isn't this nearly impossible?

Of course, it's impossible to get a perfect count. However, estimates based upon a new technique are accurate enough to provide required data for studies and restocking purposes.

The technique is called the "removal method." Here's how it works. Part of a stream is blocked off with fine-mesh nets to keep the fish from entering or leaving. This section is called the "index area." An electrical device (Electro-fisher) is used throughout the area to shock the fish. While they are temporarily stunned, biologists remove them for count, classification, weight, and measurements. Later, they are returned to the water without any harmful effects. The number of fish counted represents an index, or mathematical tool, to estimate the fish population in the rest of the stream.

What does the term "fishery management" mean?

Fishery management can best be defined by its objective: the production and maintenance of an annual yield of wild fish for recreational purposes.

The objective is implemented in three ways: (1) catch regulation, (2) population management, and (3) management of the environment.

Catches are regulated by laws that define bag limits, size limits, and closed seasons. Population management is involved in stocking streams and lakes, removing excess fish, and striking a normal balance among the different species. Management of the environment is unbelievably complex and much more difficult to attain. It comprises many measures that will improve the habitat of fish, such as pollution control and/or elimination, fish ladders, etc.

Exactly what activities come under a state's fishery management?

Habitat improvement; acquisition, development, and man-

This is how salmon were introduced successfully into the Great Lakes. These smolts, descendants of Pacific salmon (many generations removed!) were hatchery-bred locally and released in streams leading into Lake Michigan. (WISCONSIN NATURAL RESOURCES DEPT.)

agement of natural spawning areas; operation of fish hatcheries and rearing ponds for the propagation and distribution of fish; rescue of fish from lakes where they are subject to winter kill; rough-fish control by netting; lake rehabilitation, by using toxicants to reduce the population of some game species and/ or rough fish, thereby establishing the desired balance in the food chain; administration of licensed commercial fishing; and formulation of regulations governing the harvest of fish.

The objective of most states is to provide a maximum and sustained yield of fish from the waters of that state. This may mean planting fish brought from other states or the introduction of a hybrid species that may either prove valuable to the support of game fish or contribute directly to sport or commercial fishing. But the underlying objective of fishery management is to create for the angler a maximum number of satisfactory sport-fishing hours.

I've always wondered how state fish hatcheries rear game fish for restocking purposes. Where do the fish come from originally?

The propagation of game fish is a rather complex subject with many ramifications, because of the number of species and hybrids to be considered. But essentially, it begins with the egg.

During the spawning season, hatchery personnel search for schools of fish ripe with eggs and milt. The fish are netted (in some instances they are shocked electrically to stun them temporarily for handling convenience), most of the eggs are removed, and the milt (sperm) is collected from the males. The parent fish are returned immediately to their native environment.

When the eggs and milt are mixed gently, fertilization takes place in less than a minute. Then the eggs are placed in temperature-controlled incubation trays or glass containers until the fry hatch.

The juveniles are distributed in tanks big enough for feeding and development, and after they reach a certain size they are transferred into still larger tanks. Later, they will be moved to outdoor ponds for further growth and adjustment to more normal surroundings.

When they reach a size that will enable them to survive under natural conditions, they will be released into the lakes and streams throughout the state.

What does it actually cost to raise a muskie, a bass, or a panfish in a hatchery?

The Bass Research Foundation conducted a survey of hatcheries throughout the eastern United States and made the following determinations regarding the values of freshwater fishes:

Muskies top the list at $11.40 per pound. A largemouth bass costs $2.85 a pound. It takes $3.42 to raise a one-pound bluegill. Speckled perch and crappies cost $2.85 a pound. At the bottom of the list are catfish at $1.14 per pound.

Millions of muskellunge will hatch from these temperature-controlled eggs. The muskie is one of the most expensive game fishes to rear under artificial conditions; fingerlings when released will cost the state over $11 per pound. (WISCONSIN NATURAL RESOURCES DEPT.)

The survey also revealed that the most expensive freshwater fish to raise is the sturgeon, at $57 per pound. That's why caviar is so expensive!

Since experiments have proved that artificial reefs are successful attractants to saltwater fish, why don't we hear more about man-made reefs to attract freshwater fish?

You will. The idea is just beginning to catch on. Fishery biologists advocate the building of artificial reefs in freshwater lakes so that fish have a protected place where a healthy ecosystem can be maintained. This will be especially beneficial to anglers who live in heavily populated subdivisions bordering a lake. They can fish in their own backyards, and the expensive programs of constantly restocking the lake with fry can be minimized.

The most popular, and inexpensive, freshwater man-made reefs are made from interlocked rubber tires, tied in groups and sunk to the lake bottom.

While fishing in one of the commercial trout ponds in North Carolina, I noticed some trout leaping into the tumbling water that flowed from a small culvert about 5 feet above the bank. What causes trout to act this way?

Their natural instincts compel them to swim upstream to spawn or to find a more comfortable environment. It is extraordinary to see these artificially bred trout following the same instincts as those which inhabit and reproduce in a natural environment.

Even seventh-generation artificially bred pond trout possess the instinct of their ancestors—to battle their way upstream to spawn. This gravid female repeatedly attempted to reach the opening in the hatchery flow pipe. (HAL SCHARP)

If I wanted my own private fishpond, how could I build it economically?

You can obtain all kinds of free help and information from federal and state agencies. Your local game warden, too, will be happy to get you started and tell you which agencies to contact.

But first of all, before you waste your time, you'd better check your county ordinances. There just might be some regulation on the books that will give you a problem or even "sink" your project before you get started.

Write for a copy of "Building a Pond," which is available from the Office of Conservation, U.S. Dept. of Agriculture, Washington, D.C. This illustrated 14-page booklet was written by the Soil Conservation Service in response to the public's growing interest in private ponds.

As a conscientious angler, what can I do to promote conservation and assist in the perpetuation of freshwater fish?

If all anglers showed the same concern as you, then there

A conservation-minded angler demonstrates the proper way to release a fish. He grasps it firmly with *both* hands to prevent possible injury to himself or the fish.
(J. SWEDBERG, MAINE FISHERIES AND WILDLIFE)

would be no problem. Don't sell yourself short. There are several positive steps that one angler can take, and you can start by learning as much as possible about the habits of fish and the part they and their food sources play in the ecosystem.

Then you might want to join one or more of the many organizations at municipal, county, state, and federal levels that are dedicated to the same ideals. Or subscribe to periodicals whose editorial policies are directed toward conservation. If you are financially able, you can contribute personally by sponsoring research programs aimed at wildlife protection.

You can also teach other anglers by practicing good conservation methods. If every angler would release more fish, use less natural bait, and fish well within the season limits, large populations would have a better chance of surviving the onslaught that takes place when the season opens.

What is the best way to remove my hook from a fish that I want to release?

Handle your fish as little as possible. Use a wet towel or rag to hold it or, if you are using your bare hands, keep them wet. The idea here is to prevent dry contact that will damage or remove the fish's protective cover—a slimelike membrane. This slimy substance helps protect the body from a fungus attack that, given a chance to spread, could eventually kill the fish.

To remove the hook, try to slip the barb from the fish's lip by applying gentle downward and backward pressure on the hook eye. A pair of small needle-nosed pliers, or the regular pistol-grip hook removers featured in leading tackle shops, are most helpful and safer to use.

How did salmon get into the great lakes? I thought these species were confined to coastal waters and rivers only.

Your question triggers a classic example of effective, well-organized fishery management. By the middle '50s, Atlantic

Coho and Chinook salmon were introduced into the Great Lakes to reduce the growing alewife population. This Chinook reached 25 pounds in only a few years. Heavy spinning tackle and cut bait, such as smelt and alewife, are used to catch these gamesters along Chicago's rocky waterfront. (ILLINOIS DEPT. OF CONSERVATION)

alewives represented almost 90 percent of the Great Lakes' fish. The population of these undesirable migrants had exploded to such an extent that millions of them died each summer from starvation and/or lack of oxygen. When multitudes of rotten, bloated fish washed up on the beaches and shorelines, they created severe ecological and pollution problems for cities and property owners.

After intense research studies, conservation officials and biologists determined that the Pacific cohos and Chinook salmon (because of their predictable migratory patterns and extremely rapid growth rates) were logical predators for the alewife.

Therefore, in 1966, coho and Chinook salmon were introduced into areas of the Great Lakes. This, the world's largest fishery-stocking experiment, succeeded beyond anyone's expectations. The local, hatchery-bred 5-to-6-inch salmon smolts matured so rapidly that in 18 months the juveniles—after gorging themselves on a diet of alewives—averaged 16 pounds!

In further experiments steelhead and lake trout, whose longevity is far greater than that of coho and Chinook salmon, were also introduced, with smashing success.

Subsequently, the Great Lakes became one of the most productive sport fisheries in North America, and their fishermen are experiencing action comparable to that of Pacific Coast anglers.

How long can freshwater game fish usually live without food?

Depending upon their physical conditions and habitat, they can live for surprisingly long periods. Most fish can go for weeks without eating; others, for months.

Fish are able to draw upon the fat reserves stored in their bodies to sustain them during long periods of fasting. For instance, Chinook salmon exhibit astounding feats of endurance. By spring, when they head for the coastal streams to spawn, they're full of fat and vigor. During their journeys, which may take many weeks, of 800 to 2,500 miles, they refuse to eat—their sole purpose being to perform their function of perpetuating the species.

Is it true that fish always feed more just before a storm? If so, why?

Some scientists subscribe to the theory that fish become hungrier when the barometer begins to fall. On the other hand, it has also been proved that fish are more voracious feeders during some phases of the moon. When these two conditions coincide, no one can be sure what causes fish to go on a feeding spree!

There is another supposition based upon the effect of sedimentation on a fish's respiratory system. Since the sediment that hangs suspended in the water after a storm is composed of fine, sharp particles, it can irritate a fish's delicate gill structures. Therefore, if fish sense the approach of a storm, they will feed more than usual—knowing instinctively that they must restrain their respiration and locomotion and, thus, their search for food, until the sediment settles to the bottom and the water returns to its natural clarity.

In general, how often do freshwater fish feed, and do they follow some kind of schedule or regimen?

No. The appetites of freshwater fish vary according to the water temperature. There could be a lot of food available, but if the water is too warm or too cold, fish will refuse to feed. Their digestive processes slow down in direct proportion to unsuitable temperatures, and they become inactive. Even the temperaments of predaceous species change when uncomfortable conditions exist.

But when water temperatures are ideal, fish's appetites will sharpen and they will feed more than once every day as their digestive processes speed up. It is important to know not only how to fish, but *when* to fish.

What are the ideal water temperatures for some of the freshwater game fishes?

According to ichthyologists, the ideal temperature ranges for the following fish are: brook trout, 53–65 degrees; largemouth bass, 68–75 degrees; smallmouth bass, 65–71 degrees; walleyes 60–70 degrees; muskellunge, 60–70 degrees; northern pike, 50–70 degrees; lake trout, 40–55 degrees; Atlantic salmon, 57–61 degrees; Pacific salmon, 53–55 degrees.

Of course, fish can be caught in water temperatures outside these readings, but not often.

Do game fish think? Why is it that some species seem to be smarter than others?

Fish do not have the sophisticated reasoning abilities that the higher orders of animals possess. They do have memories (although very short), but they cannot reason things out. Fish act strictly by instinct, employing their full complement of sensory equipment. This involves using their olfactory, auditory, tactile, and visual senses to locate food and to escape from predators.

Like most wildlife, fish are basically lazy, intent only upon seeking food, comfort, and breeding opportunities.

Many fish are curious, so on the basis of this premise, anglers who learn how to excite a fish's curiosity will be well rewarded.

Do fish feel pain? My wife and kids look upon me with disgust when I insert a hook into a live, struggling bait fish.

Your family probably feel more pain than the bait. Fish and shrimp are in a lower class of animals and do not possess the sophisticated nervous system the higher orders have. If any pain is felt by fish, it is very little. They are not conditioned physiologically or consciously to feel pain as we know and understand it.

How sensitive are fish to colors? Can they actually distinguish one from another?

Yes, fish are definitely sensitive to colors, and they *can* distinguish one from another—but only under the best conditions. Other factors such as depth, light, and water clarity affect their reactions by distorting the color of a lure.

Most fish's eyes are well developed and suited to their environment. Although they are basically nearsighted, they have a visual field of about 190 degrees on each side, so that few close objects escape their notice.

You must try to select your lure according to the water conditions, but also keep in mind the appetite and personality of your quarry. Another important factor to consider is the movement you impart to your lure. If a fast retrieve doesn't work, try a slow one. Trial and error with colors and movements is the best way to discover a productive lure.

Is there any truth to the theory that fish are able to detect human scent clinging to the tackle and bait? If so, does it make them wary?

Since fish have exceptionally keen olfactory equipment, it is possible that they can detect the scent of humans and find it so objectionable that they might refuse the bait.

Rather than take a chance that perspiration, insect-repellent, gasoline, or lubricating-oil scent will "turn a fish off," take a leaf from the old-timers' book and wash your hands before you handle tackle and bait.

How do biologists determine the age of a fish?

They do this by counting the rings on the fish's scales. Except for a few species, all fish have scales, but some are so small that they must be magnified to make it possible to count the rings.

Narrow rings indicate years of little growth, and wide rings show rapid growth when food was more abundant. By counting all the rings you can estimate not only the fish's age but also its rate of growth.

Can fish hear, and do sounds frighten them away?

Yes, they can hear very well. However, sounds made above and out of the water have little effect. A few feet of water between the fish and the emitting source of sound help serve as insulation.

Sound detection plays an important role in a fish's survival. Unlike those of most land animals, the hearing organs of a fish are made up of inner ears specifically designed for sound reception and the detection of vibrations underwater. The "ears" are located in the skull and also function to maintain a fish's equilibrium.

Most sounds made underwater will frighten a fish away. A good example is the noisy fisherman who bumps the side or the bottom of a boat with his feet or oars. These sudden noises create vibrations in the water that scare fish hundreds of feet away.

There are, however, some sounds that will attract many species of game fish. These sounds are in a special frequency range that appeals to the fish's curiosity. Electronic-gear manufacturers are experimenting continually with highly sophisticated fish-attraction apparatus that will also appeal to the fisherman.

What happens to fish when lightning strikes the water?

All living creatures caught on the surface in the direct path of a discharge will be either killed or injured—depending upon the strength of the discharge and the distance from the source. In other words, the greater the distance from the origin of the lightning to the fish, the less harm is done.

Although there is little damage when lightning hits small streams and ponds, the fish in large bodies of water such as huge reservoirs and the Great Lakes are almost as vulnerable as saltwater species.

From a physiological standpoint, what takes place in a fish when it is confronted by a bait or pursues a meal?

Assuming that the fish is hungry, several organs, triggered by instinct, begin to function. Depending upon environment, water conditions, and the manner in which a bait or meal is offered, a fish locates its food via one organ or a combination of organs. For example, a live, struggling bait impaled upon a hook in relatively clear water will attract a fish who has (1) seen it, (2) heard its emission of distress sounds, (2) smelled it, and (4) felt it with his lateral line system—but not necessarily in that order.

Furthermore, after seeing the bait, some fish will strike it without hesitation only to satisfy their curiosity or irascibility. Others may approach a bait, doubt its authenticity, and refuse it. The real trick, therefore, is to make the fish want it and want it badly enough to strike—regardless of the bait's genuineness. All of this depends upon the quality or kind of bait and the manner in which it is presented. And, last, a lot of patience is required.

What is the function of a fish's air bladder?

A fish's air (or swim) bladder is a highly sophisticated organ that has various functions among different species. It is a capillary-lined, gas-filled, airtight, membranelike chamber located between the stomach and the backbone. Its actual position depends upon the fish's anatomy and swimming characteristics. Because it is located near the fish's center of gravity and buoyancy, it maintains stability and assists in locomotion. By inflating or deflating its bladder, a fish is able to maintain proper buoyancy at different water depths. Since the density of fresh water is less than that of salt, freshwater fishes possess larger air bladders than saltwater species.

In some species, the bladder is connected to the ears by tubes. It acts as a microphone, resonating chamber, and amplifier by picking up vibrations in the water and transmitting them to the ears. Several species use their air bladders to emit sounds for mating purposes.

Does artificial light from a lantern or other illuminating device attract game fish?

Some game fish are frightened, others are attracted, and several are dazed by it. Bass are usually frightened by any kind of light, while muskies and pike appear to be dazed. Salmon have been found to be stupefied by light—as demonstrated by the Indians who use lights on their boats when spearing salmon commercially. Trout are easily attracted to a light, especially when they feed on the insects that are drawn to it.

In some states the use of a light to attract fish is illegal, so anglers should check their state game laws first.

In any event, using a light doesn't appeal to the majority of anglers, since its application suggests poor sportsmanship.

What are the tiny round black spots found in the flesh of some fish? Are they caused by some disease that might injure our health if we eat them?

Black spots such as you describe are caused by an immature form of parasitic flatworm. Some species of fish contain more than others. Usually, those fish which spend a good part of their lives in shallow water are more apt to come into contact with the parasite than those which inhabit deep water.

The adult, egg-laying form is found in the intestinal tract of a common carrier, such as the belted kingfisher. The eggs are passed from the bird into the water, where they subsequently hatch. The larval forms burrow into several species of snails, where full development takes place. Later, as adults, they leave the snails and search for a fish to serve as a host to provide sustenance. As they penetrate the fish's flesh, the fish forms a sac of tissue to wall off the worm from direct contact with its flesh. It is the sacs that make the telltale black spots.

Although the spots are unsightly, the fish are edible. Normal cooking processes destroy all the parasites, so that they cause no harm.

What is the largest freshwater fish in the world, and where is it found?

The sturgeon. There are about 16 species in the sturgeon

family, an even more primitive and much older fish than the herring or trout. One species that inhabits the Amur River of northern Asia sometimes grows over 12 feet long and often weighs over 2,000 pounds.

Other species are found in Europe and America. Five- and six-hundred-pounders have been caught in Washington and Oregon. Sturgeons are well known for their roe, which is prized as caviar. The lake sturgeon is the best-known American species and is the largest fish in the Great Lakes. This species reaches 6 feet in length and will weigh 100 pounds or over.

I can understand the principle of sportsmanship—release a fish so it can fight again another day—but what has this to do with conservation?

Plenty. If you catch a female salmon, bass, or muskie full of roe (it happens during the open season) and release it, you will be contributing to the perpetuation of the species. Your release, multiplied by thousands of others every year, reflects a great attitude toward conservation *and* sportsmanship.

If a fish is too big or dangerous to handle, how can I release it safely with a minimum of injury to the fish?

Use a standard release gaff hook and gaff your fish only in the lower jaw. Slip the gaff slowly into the fish's mouth and make your penetration in the thin connective tissue that holds the tongue to the mandible. Or you may find it easier to run your gaff into the lower jaw from the outside.

If netting or gaffing isn't practical, leave the fish in the water, draw it up close, and snip the leader as close to the hook as possible. Eventually, the hook will deteriorate from contact with the fish's body acids.

At least once in the life of every angler, he catches a fish with someone else's hook in its stomach or mouth. This partially deteriorated hook obviously had not affected the fish's health, since it was hooked again while feeding!

I've heard that anglers who release their fish give them artificial respiration. What, exactly, do they do?

Yes, conservation-minded anglers who prefer to release their quarry do employ first aid to ensure the fish's chances of survival.

However, artificial respiration is usually given only to a fish that has expended all its energy during the battle. It will die soon after being released unless you give it a little help.

The method is simple. Place your hand, or hands, underneath the fish's belly and support it for a few minutes in the water. It's important that you try to increase its oxygen intake by moving the fish slowly back and forth. This movement forces water into its mouth and out through the gills. Since a fish's gills are the equivalent of an air-breathing animal's lungs, they are sensitive and easily injured. A fish should never be held by its gill covers unless you intend to keep it.

I think I have a reasonable knowledge of *how* to catch fish. But now I'd like to know *where* to fish and *what* the rules and regulations are in specific locales. Any suggestions?

Write to the fish-and-game commission in the capital city of the state where you're planning to fish. Although in some states the commissions may be known by other titles, your letter will eventually reach the right place.

You'll be amazed at the amount of information that some of these fish-conscious agencies put out. In some instances there may be a small handling charge, but it's well worth it. The material covers the what, where, when, and how on fishing and often includes maps, survey figures, and locations of tackle shops, boat ramps, marina facilities, and accommodations.

What are the objectives of the Sport Fishing Institute? Is membership open to the public?

The Sport Fishing Institute, organized in 1949 by a group of fishing manufacturers, has the following objectives:

1. To promote and assist in conservation, development, and wise utilization of our national recreational fisheries resources.
2. To advance and encourage the development and application of all branches of fishery research and management.
3. To collect, evaluate, and publish all information of value to advance fishery science and the sport of fishing.
4. To assist existing educational institutions in the training of personnel in fisheries science and management.
5. To encourage a wider participation in sport fishing through the distribution of information pertaining to its health and recreational values.
6. To assist and encourage cooperative effort among all existing conservation organizations.

Yes, its membership is open to the public. For details about joining and for more information about how the organization operates, write to

Sport Fishing Institute
608 13th Street, N.W.
Washington, D.C. 20005

In what section of the United States will I find the most species of freshwater game fish?

For diversity, it's hard to beat Wisconsin, Minnesota, and Michigan. All three states have muskies, northerns, bass, trout, walleyes, catfish, and most members of the panfish family. You can also catch cohos, Chinook salmon, and steelhead trout in Lake Superior, Lake Michigan, and their tributaries.

Why do northern fish seem sluggish during the winter months? Do they hibernate?

They are not as active, nor do they feed as much, as they do during the rest of the year. However, they do eat just enough to sustain life.

Since fish are cold-blooded creatures, their metabolic rates are controlled by the environment in which they live and, specifically, by water temperature. Changes in temperature will alter their heart rates and, in turn, slow their metabolism and/or rate of digestion. Therefore, cool or warm water can affect their appetites and slow their digestive processes. This produces a stuporous state, which may give an angler the impression that the lake is fished out or that the fish are hibernating. However, they are still able to carry out their physiological functions in the winter months.

Why are freshwater fish cheaper to mount than saltwater fish? How much does each cost?

According to Archie Phillips, taxidermist of the "nation's largest bass studio," Fairfield, Alabama, size doesn't mean much in the figuring of costs for mounting some fish species. He will do bass of any size (2 pounds or 20), panfish, etc., for $45. These species have heavy, coarse skins that make them easier to handle and process.

However, striped bass and trout cost about 50 cents an inch, or about $55 minimum.

Saltwater fish cost about $3.75 an inch, or $68 minimum. The skins of saltwater fish are more delicate and difficult to process, and mounting them is, therefore, more expensive.

Are there any differences between the freshwater sheepshead and the saltwater sheepshead? If so, what are they?

Yes, indeed, they are two completely unrelated species. The freshwater sheepshead is also known as a drum or "gaspergow" and belongs to the croaker family. Although he may weigh as much as 35 pounds, he is not considered a desirable food fish.

The saltwater sheepshead is a member of the porgy family.

Because they are handsomely marked with black vertical stripes and are adept at stealing bait, saltwater sheepshead are often called "convict fish"! They average about 2 pounds, often tip the scales at 5 or 6 pounds, and are excellent table fare. They are found chiefly in the inshore waters of the southeastern and Gulf coasts of the United States.

How many species of freshwater minnows are there?

Over 200 species. Popular bait species are dace, skinner, chase, and chub.

Are there any freshwater fish that will deliberately attack man?

The piranhas, or "cannibal fish," found in several South American rivers have been responsible for the deaths of many natives and animals. Although the critters may not weigh more than a few pounds, they travel in huge schools attacking and consuming anything that moves. They possess exceptionally strong jaws filled with many sharp, triangular teeth and are capable of reducing a full-size cow to a skeleton in minutes.

This treacherous species could thrive in the fresh waters of the southern United States but (thank heaven!) it's illegal to transport, import, or raise them except for municipal exhibits.

The alligator gar found in the lower Mississippi Valley region is a toothy villain that grows to 9 feet in length and reaches 150 pounds. There are several reported cases of attacks upon people, none of which were fatal.

Although the Lake Nicaragua shark (*Carcharhinus nicaraguensis*) is a freshwater species, it is not a true bony fish. In the lakes and rivers of Central and South America, this species has been responsible for many fatal attacks upon people.

What is the official rod-and-reel world's record for a freshwater fish?

According to records compiled by *Field & Stream*, the largest fish was a white sturgeon that weighed 360 pounds. It was caught in the Snake River, Idaho, in 1956.

The runner-up was an alligator gar that weighed 279 pounds, caught in the Rio Grande River, Texas, in 1951.

Index